Sheep in Wolves' Clothing

Hamewith Books

Hamewith Books celebrate our living God—he who dwells with and within us and who longs to heal us. These books name the idolatries that are rampant today, and they show how healing can take place. After repentance and forgiveness of sin, healing abounds for spirit, soul, and body. *Hamewith* is a Scottish word meaning "at home within" or "the road home," and Hamewith Books seek to help us reclaim the full Judeo-Christian view of reality.

Mario Bergner, *Setting Love in Order: Hope and Healing for the Homosexual*

Leanne Payne, *Crisis in Masculinity*

Leanne Payne, *The Broken Image: Restoring Personal Wholeness through Healing Prayer*

Leanne Payne, *Healing Homosexuality*

Leanne Payne, *The Healing Presence: Curing the Soul through Union with Christ*

Leanne Payne, *Listening Prayer: Learning to Hear God's Voice and Keep a Prayer Journal*

Leanne Payne, *Real Presence: The Glory of Christ with Us and within Us*

Leanne Payne, *Restoring the Christian Soul: Overcoming Barriers to Completion in Christ through Healing Prayer*

Jeffrey Satinover, M.D., *Homosexuality and the Politics of Truth*

Sheep in Wolves' Clothing

How Unseen Need Destroys Friendship and Community and What to Do about It

Second Edition

Valerie J. McIntyre

Foreword by Leanne Payne

A Hamewith Book

Baker Books
A Division of Baker Book House Co
Grand Rapids, Michigan 49516

Published by Baker Books
a division of Baker Book House Company
P.O. Box 6287, Grand Rapids, MI 49516-6287

Previously published in 1996 by Pastoral Care Ministries

Printed in the United States of America

Library of Congress Cataloging-in-Publication Data

McIntyre, Valerie J.
   Sheep in wolves' clothing : how unseen need destroys friendship and community and what to do about it / Valerie J. McIntyre ; foreword by Leanne Payne.
      p.   cm.
   "A Hamewith book."
   Includes bibliographical references.
   ISBN 0-8010-5883-X (pbk.)
     1. Conflict management—Religious aspects—Christianity. 2. Transference (Psychology)—Religious aspects—Christianity. I. Title.
BV4597.53.C58M38   1999
2553.5'2—dc21   98-50492

For current information about all releases from Baker Book House, visit our web site:

http://www.bakerbooks.com

For information about Pastoral Care Ministries, visit PCM's web site:
www.LeannePayneNews.com

To Charis,

an emblem of God's grace to me

Contents

Foreword

*I*n *Sheep in Wolves' Clothing* Valerie McIntyre has given us an extraordinarily important book that can bring healing to leaders and laypeople alike. Her insights on the psychological and spiritual malady that psychologists refer to as transference are simply groundbreaking.

This is not because she has superior technical and psychological knowledge about the ins and outs of transference, projection, splitting, and so on, although she does have sufficient understanding. Rather, her perceptions are illuminated because she lived out a painful personal experience of transference in the presence of God, placing all the motions of her soul in the full light of the Scriptures. In obedience to God she made the right choices, godly ones that strike at the heart of human pride.

Valerie desired to know God and his truth. Bringing herself in line with his reality—with the way things really are—she gained spiritual knowledge of the motions of the wounded soul. Here, with great and piercing clarity, she shares her story and her understanding. We are all the grateful recipients of her courageous honesty.

Equipment for the Battle

A soul traumatized by its own or another's sinfulness can repress or split off from its sin and woundedness. Later, this split-off "badness" is projected onto others. When the dynamics are correctly perceived and spread out in the light of truth, a transference in which this diseased matter from the unconscious surfaces becomes worth its weight in gold, despite the accompanying pain. As the painful memories and the denial mechanisms that have repressed them are dealt with, healing comes.

But those who fail to acknowledge the situation and face the underlying issues are unable to resolve their difficulty. It is then that we see Christian people acting as wolves among God's flock, and we find ourselves contending with sheep in wolves' clothing. Unfortunately this seems to be happening more and more, due to the breakup of homes and the loss of stable parenting.

We have come to term those liable to receive such transferences "high transference liabilities." When they are the object of a transference, needy individuals will superidealize them at first, seeing them as totally good and without flaw. But then as healing starts and the repressed memories and feelings emerge, they project the diseased matter onto the object of their transference, whom they then perceive as all bad. Envy, slander, and lies commonly accompany such a transference.

If we do not understand what is really happening in such cases, the slanderous lies that begin to circulate will destroy our unity and God's work of renewal in our midst. I have had plenty of opportunity to lament the fact that I am a "high transference liability," and had I not come to understand these dynamics, I would perhaps no longer be in ministry. Because I am a motherly woman and move out strongly in healing prayer for primitive injuries, I receive some of the worst.

To comprehend what Valerie lays out in this book, and to discern and connect this understanding to the spiritual warfare swirling about in the body of Christ today, is to be strengthened in "the gift of battle." As Oswald Chambers has said, "we are not sent to battle for God, but to be used by God in His battlings." I trust that *Sheep in Wolves' Clothing* will provide an important piece of armament in our struggle, helping us to resist and remain standing when the battle is won.

—Leanne Payne

Acknowledgments

ing Solomon once wrote, "Counsel in the heart of a man is like water in a deep well, but a man of understanding will draw it out" (Proverbs 20:5, AMP). I am truly grateful to Leanne Payne who, long before I could see it, perceived that there was water in the well of my heart which, if it could be drawn up, would satisfy the thirst of many in need of insight regarding transference.

Special thanks are also due to Rev. Mario Bergner for the *way* he tells his story at Pastoral Care Ministry schools. His example of honesty has inspired courage in me—first to write out my story truthfully in the presence of God, and then to share it publicly. Had I not taken those first steps, this book would not have been written.

Also, I have found the strength to finish this project from the friendship and prayer support of Rev. Bob and Connie Boerner, John Fawcett, Cindy Keuchenberg, Karen Miller, Eirik and Jeanne Olsen, Amy Boucher Pye, Dr. Jeffrey Satinover, and Helen Solem.

Finally, I am especially grateful to my husband, Mark, for the many meaningful discussions we have had about the subject.

Introduction

*I*n our day many pastors have relinquished their hope for loving, holy relationships with the people in their congregations. Instead they have settled for just surviving. And rather than glorying in the way the kingdom of God moves forward as they—hand in hand with their flock—follow the Great Shepherd, they have come to expect their churches to be embroiled in petty controversies or even vicious conflicts.

In the midst of this pain and confusion many ministers have searched to make sense of the disappointment they have experienced. A few have chosen to leave the ministry. Others have lowered their expectations. And still others have relinquished themselves to being puppets for the factious groups that run many churches.

Many of the conflicts that divide churches and press clergy out of the ministry are related to the unrecognized dynamics of *transference*. This term, which is germane to the world of counselors, psychologists, and doctors, refers to the way the experiences, memories, and other factors from a person's past can be transferred into the present in a way that brings great confusion. But the role that this dynamic plays in church conflicts is generally not understood. And thus, in the words of the prophet Hosea, God's people are being "destroyed from lack of knowledge" (Hosea 4:6, NASB).

Churches are not the only place where transference occurs: It can be found between one friend and another, between an employee and his boss, between a person and her spiritual mentor. Leaders, in particular, tend to be targets of transference.

But whatever the situation, everyone suffers when transference goes unrecognized. The unresolved issues from the past continue to leave their mark on the present, affecting the person in particular and increasingly those with whom he or she comes into contact.

When transference becomes destructive to pastors, innocent bystanders are left without their shepherd—or with one who is too fearful to lead effectively. The ministers and their families can be deeply hurt. The church is thrown into confusion and even gossip, malice, and deception.

And, sadly, those who are at the center of the problem, the ones in transference, fail to get the help they need. The sheep in wolves' clothing are never divested of their loathsome furry garments. They remain wrapped up in their sin and pain.

But there is good news: The light of understanding can shine into these situations as soon as the dynamic of transference is identified. And everyone involved can receive God's healing through the appropriation of the central reality of our faith, the death and resurrection of Christ.

Through the confession of sin, the power of forgiveness, and the healing virtue of the Holy Spirit, the objects of transference can be restored to joy. And through the same, those suffering in transference can be helped out of their wolf skins and into their true identity as sons and daughters of God.

We will be looking at the dynamics of transference and how it affects people in and out of church. In part 1 we will explore the notion of transference itself, beginning with my own story in chapter 1. In chapter 2 we move to definitions of transference and related terms, and in chapter 3 to the dynamics of replayed memories. We continue the examination of childhood and infancy in chapter 4. And in chapter 5 we will look at the relationship between repression, pride, and self-deception.

In part 2 we turn to the hallmarks of transference in the church. Chapters 6, 7, and 8 each explore specific kinds of transference: overt and litigious, covert and factious, and vicarious, respectively. These kinds of transference are all affected by spiritual battle, the subject of chapter 9.

Part 3 concerns the remedy for transference. In chapter 10 we will explore various measures and actions to take when dealing with transference, and in chapter 11 certain traps to avoid. Chapter 12 is written for all those who suspect that they themselves are in a transference; it points the way toward a healing release. We conclude with a happy ending, for God has given us the resources with which to be free of the pain and confusion brought about by transferences.

PART 1

Understanding Transference

1

My Story

A number of years ago I had what I then thought was the perfect friendship. Cindy was the first female peer with whom I fully identified, a true "kindred spirit." I had met her at Wheaton College (in a suburb outside of Chicago) when we both served on the same leadership team for a vibrant student fellowship.

We spent a lot of time together, not only on the leadership team but away from school as well. Cindy welcomed me into her grandparents' home for various weekend visits and also into the life of her church. But after about eight months our relationship began to sour.

I can see now elements in the friendship that revealed emotional dependency, or "bentness." For instance, I remember vividly a conversation Cindy and I had after praying together one evening. She commented, "Sometimes when we pray together, I'm not sure whether I'm myself or whether I'm you."

I acknowledged that I also felt this odd absence of personal boundaries. That night I lay awake for hours, confused by my conflicting emotions. I longed for this kind of "oneness" but at the same time felt alarmed, certain that something was terribly wrong.

But emotional dependency was not the only problem, for I envied Cindy. In particular I was jealous of her amazing capacity to be fully alive—a state of being I lacked. Cindy was unhindered by inhibition and could freely express her thoughts and feelings, devotion to God, and love for animals, children, and her friends. I would admire this freedom one moment and in the next turn and subtly belittle her for it.

Changing Perceptions

In the middle of the spring semester Cindy decided quite abruptly to withdraw from Wheaton and return home to complete her degree at a local university. I wasn't sure her decision was sound, and in fact I began to obsess over the rightness or wrongness of it. My emotional reaction to her choice was completely out of proportion to the actual situation, especially my feelings of rejection, anger, and grief. I made a huge effort to hide these emotions when I was with Cindy.

Over the next year our friendship continued by letters, phone calls, and an occasional visit. But my feelings of anger, envy, and jealousy continued to grow in intensity. I was mildly depressed most of the time and could not stop thinking about Cindy's decision to leave Wheaton. With this constant mental obsession I found academic work quite difficult.

During this time the way I viewed Cindy had changed. Before her move I had admired her spiritual sensitivity and giftedness; now I imagined that her relationship with God was deteriorating and that her other friendships were unhealthy. Nonetheless, I was very jealous of those friendships and was frustrated and unhappy unless I had her exclusive attention.

I also began to perceive Cindy as being like my mother. When a friend asked me what the similarity was, I could not articulate any objective answer. I was unable to see it at the time, but Cindy is actually very unlike my mother, having great strengths and personal resources in areas where my mother is lacking.

Oddly, these troubling thoughts and feelings would entirely disappear whenever I was actually with Cindy; when we were together I truly enjoyed her friendship. But these emotions would return just before we parted, or the next day.

The Monster in My Imagination

It wasn't long before I began to look at my relationship with Cindy as a "conflict" that needed "resolution and reconciliation." I began to imagine a confrontation based on Matthew 18:15–17 in which I would "go and show her, just between the two of us, her faults." I would call her to account for all the ways she had failed the Scriptures and injured me. What I wanted most was for her to acknowledge and apologize for her part in our "conflict."

Finally I wrote a letter in my attempt to confront Cindy. I told her that I did not expect her to be perfect; I just wanted her to admit her "faults" and the ways she had "hurt" me. But her response, soon after she received my letter, was neither what I expected nor what I had hoped for.

Cindy called me on the phone and informed me that she would not be going to the wedding of a mutual friend that we had planned to attend together. When I heard this news I became intensely angry—so angry that it frightened me. Never before had I felt such rage against another. All my previously hidden negative feelings toward Cindy were now out in the open.

She endured my angry outburst and then responded to my letter by pointing out—accurately—that "we" were not having a conflict; it existed only in my point of view. She also told me that my expectations of her and the friendship were unrealistic and unhealthy, and that my accusations were simply untrue.

When I did not get the apologetic response I wanted from Cindy my feelings of anger and hurt intensified. She became more and more of a monster in my imagination.

I became increasingly frustrated with her and frequently discussed my feelings with my roommate and the leadership team of which Cindy had been a part. I must have been persuasive as I presented my case against her, because our mutual friends all adopted my point of view. In fact, they thought more highly of me for being such a faithful friend to someone so difficult. This is precisely how I viewed the situation, and I resorted to gossip and slander to ensure the solidarity of my friends.

"Choose Humility"

But a week after the phone call when I truly quieted my heart before God, I knew that Cindy was right. In one journal entry during that time I wrote out Proverbs 22:4: "The reward for humility and fear of the LORD is riches and honor and life" (NRSV). Through this passage of Scripture the Lord was asking me to choose the way of humility. While warning me that my pride placed me in great danger, he was also promising to bless me if I would humble myself.

I finally began to acknowledge my confusion and to confess my sins, asking for God's insight and cleansing. Even without fully understanding my situation, I sensed the great spiritual and psychological danger I was in. Thankfully, I had walked with the Lord long enough to know that I could trust him to intervene.

On a visit to my hometown, I sought out the one person I hoped could help me. She, however, was unavailable. I continued to struggle alone before the Lord and then received a letter from Cindy. For her own safety, she wrote, she needed to sever the friendship for an indefinite period of time. She asked me not to communicate with her in any way or form.

In response to Cindy's letter I felt self-pity and frustration: My initial repentance had not "fixed" the relationship. Later I was humbled to realize that even my repentance was partly an attempt to manipulate both Cindy and God into preserving this friendship. I clung to Cindy—or to my idea of Cindy—as though I couldn't live without her.

Exhortation but Comfort

Almost despairing, I packed up my Bible, prayer-journal, and guitar and returned to Chicago to begin summer work at a rescue mission. I knew no one there and felt vulnerable and lonely. My days were spent in the soup kitchen and among the homeless, most of whom were chronically mentally ill. Working among them provided, ironically, a healthy venue from which I could look outside myself in the midst of my internal suffering.

In the evenings and on the weekends I cried out to God with all my heart. I began searching the Scriptures, worshiping and listening to God, and he gave me the specific insight I needed.

Through my prayerful study of the Bible I began to understand the principles behind my experience of transference, although I lacked an understanding of the term at the time.[1] For example, I came to understand my idolatry toward Cindy, along with the need to renounce it, through the Scriptures' clear teaching on idolatry. Likewise, God's holy Word exhorted me to take responsibility for my own sin and to seek his forgiveness. And I found in Isaiah's comforting prophecy the assurance that the Lord was waiting to take up my suffering into himself.[2]

I began to understand that the pain I was feeling had nothing to do with Cindy, and that my obsessive thinking and praying about her had to stop. This discipline proved very difficult, and some days I was more successful than others.

But I was given unexpected motivation to overcome my unhealthy thought patterns through my conversations with the mentally ill people at the shelter. It was amazing—and frightening—to realize how many of these people were stuck in a similar pattern of obsessive thinking. At times I felt quite a kinship with them!

A Man and His Horse

One man in particular brought this reality home to me—a middle-aged African American who had been living on the streets and in shelters for several years. He stood out from the crowd of homeless men for several reasons. First, being about six feet, six inches tall, he stood head and shoulders above the rest. He also made a special effort to keep his appearance neat by shaving every day and by wearing a suit and tie. As his suits were donated, however, they all were of the dated polyester variety and never fit him properly. Typically the ends of his sleeves and pants were about four inches shy of the needed length.

In addition to his appearance, he was different from the others because of his behavior. A loner, he often stood in the corner muttering to himself and appearing to carry on a conversation with an imaginary person. He used his hands demonstratively as he spoke, occasionally becoming angry with this companion or sharing a good laugh. He had a reputation among the workers at the shelter as being gentle and painfully shy.

After watching him for a week I ventured over to his corner, introduced myself, and asked for his name. He seemed reluctant to talk and refused to tell me his name. I took his cues and went back to washing the dinner dishes.

Later, as I was pouring coffee and handing out donuts, he approached me and called me by name: "Hi, Valerie! My name is Will Rogers and this is my horse," he said as he gestured toward his invisible companion. "He don't like coffee, but he'd be mighty grateful for one or two of them donuts."

I laughed and obliged him by handing over four donuts. As he thanked me his face opened up into an extraordinary smile that seemed to light up his whole body. A little later I saw him alone at a table, pretending to shoot his stack of donuts with an imaginary gun and then offering each one to his horse. He'd shrug his shoulders, shake his head, and finally eat it himself. Later I learned that "Will" had a real name, Lee.

After that night I made an effort to talk to Lee. And as the weeks passed he told me much of his life story and I told him some of mine. Soon I learned that Lee loved God and tried his best to relate to him even in his unreal world of cowboys and Indians.

In one conversation, when I was feeling especially sorry for myself and angry with Cindy, I told Lee about the difficulties I was having. Looking at me with eyes full of sympathy, he shook his head in disgust and said, "Valerie, I know just what you're going though. My friends do me the same way!"

He then embarked on a long tirade about his failed relationships. By the end of the conversation I saw plainly how the kind of twisted thinking that I was indulging in where Cindy was concerned was all too similar to the stuff of his mental illness. I also realized that the consequences could be grave if I failed to press through to reality in this situation. Jesus used this precious, pitiful man to motivate me to cry out to God with my whole heart for the healing that I needed.

Disciplines of Healing

A few weeks into the summer, I received an extremely helpful letter from a woman who was a leader in Cindy's church, whom we both respected. Her words were strong but kind as she simply pointed me to Jesus as the only One who could restore my soul. She did not sympathize with my sin or attempt to explain my problem psychologically.

With this letter I knew that Cindy had the support of her church leaders, and that they would stand with her if I tried to contact her against her wishes. The authority of the church was behind the boundaries she had set up between us, boundaries that helped turn my attention away from her to the deeper issues I needed to face.

I continually submitted my thoughts to God in prayer, asking him to fill my mind with his truth and peace. Quickly my mental habits began to return to normal, even though emotionally I did not feel better. In fact, bringing my thoughts under control seemed to intensify my emotional and physical duress. Later I understood that my obsessive thinking had been a defense, a distraction from facing the real pain that was coming up in my soul and body. Through controlling my thoughts by submitting them to the Lord this defense was dismantled.

I lost my appetite completely and always felt slightly nauseated. That summer I lost about thirty pounds, most of which I had gained in the previous twelve months when I was more mildly depressed; it took a full year and a half for my appetite to return to normal. I also felt a great deal of physical anxiety and tenseness throughout my body, but especially in my lower back, hips, shoulders, and jaws. Although I experienced moments of release from this physical discomfort, it was fairly constant then and has recurred periodically.

On some days, when I quieted myself in the Lord's presence, an unbearable amount of emotional pain would surface. I remember asking, "Lord, has anyone ever died of this condition?"

When I was hurting, I would be tempted to return to my old obsessive thinking rather than to face the pain. But here again, it was as though I had a choice to make: "What will you do with your sin and your sorrow?"

When I chose to suffer honestly before God, looking only to Jesus on the cross to bear my sin and pain, I found him lifting that measure of anguish from me and taking it into himself. Sometimes I had sensory experiences of God's presence, feeling myself cradled in a warm, loving embrace or hearing lullabies.

Standing in Truth

In my prayer times, all kinds of diseased thoughts, feelings, and images began to float up into my conscious mind from unconscious levels. Writing out these thoughts and feelings, I listened for God to speak objective truth to me through the Scriptures. I stood in the truth I heard with all my might.

Still, at times I could not sort through what was false and stand in what was true. In those moments I sensed what seemed to be a dark presence with me, one that was intent on getting me to accept as fact all manner of untruth about myself, others, and God. My thoughts were preoccupied with slanderous accusations, particularly against Cindy.

Certain that I was in some measure demonized or severely oppressed, I pleaded with God to help me win this battle. In answer to my prayer I received two important insights. First was the crystal-clear understanding that the oppression had partly occurred because I had given Cindy an idolatrous place in my heart. My idolatry of Cindy had formed early in the relationship. Not only did I idealize her virtues and spirituality, but I wrongly looked to her, rather than God, to meet my deep emotional needs.

This sinful way of relating to Cindy had opened the door to demonic oppression.[3] The affliction came in the form of intrusions into my thoughts (slanderous accusations against Cindy) and intensified my own confused feelings about her. As demonic misinformation about Cindy intermingled with my own diseased feelings, horrific caricatures of her formed in my imagination and my perception of her moved further and further from reality.

Once I realized what was happening, I was led to renounce the idols of my heart, actually renouncing the idol-god "Cindy" by name.

The second insight I received was that to be freed from the oppression, I had to name and repent of my sins. Though I truly loved Cindy as a friend, I also felt intense malice toward her. I began to understand the ways I had sinned against her: I had chosen to believe both my irrational perceptions of Cindy and the dark demonic lies, speaking them out to others in gossip and slander.

Further, when I forcefully faced Cindy with my false accusations and demanded that she "own her part of the problem," I was asking her to believe these lies, even as I had. And I had deceived others around me, disguising my carnal rage under a mask of victimization and drawing others into my sin against her.

When I confessed my sins and renounced my idolatry, the oppression lifted. The confusion in my thinking between my mother and Cindy also began to clear up, and I began to see both of them objectively.

Had I lost this battle for truth, believing the lies and distortions that bombarded my mind, I would have spiraled down into mental illness. I likely would have lost my faith and with it any hope of becoming the person God had intended for me to be. And I would have been unable to move forward in all that God has given me to do.

At the end of that summer I was more certain than ever before of God's love for me—and frightfully aware of my own capacity for sin and evil. For several months I was afraid of getting close to anyone, believing myself dangerous to have as a friend.

One of the most unusual consequences of this intense summer was a change in my physical appearance. A few days after returning to Wheaton for the new semester I had my senior picture taken. When it arrived in the mail I honestly thought the company had mistakenly sent someone else's picture. The feminine quality of my features literally shocked me.

A few weeks into the fall semester I received another surprise—a phone call from Cindy. Believing I had thoroughly destroyed the friendship, I had given up any hope of speaking to her again.

In this first call I was hesitant to talk about what had happened for fear of relapsing into diseased patterns of thought. Instead I simply told her that I had sinned against her in innumerable ways, some of which I couldn't articulate even if I tried. She was fully willing to forgive me. Over several years trust was restored, and the gift of our friendship has been preserved.

Gaining Objectivity

I now understand that over this period of eighteen months I experienced a transference related to the deprivations of my early infancy and childhood. Although on occasion I feel the old anxiety, which I have come to understand as infantile separation anxiety, I have never again suffered with the same intensity. Thoughts and feelings that are rooted in infantile deprivation and then projected or transferred onto others have a peculiar quality and thus have become easier to identify. For this I'm deeply grateful to God.

I have also learned to pray about my transferences onto others. Anytime I suspect I am transferring onto another person, I bring the matter before the Lord in prayer. I first ask his help in naming exactly what I am feeling. Then I ask for insight into why I have associated the present situation with something from my past. I have also found it helpful to talk and pray over the matter with a trusted Christian friend.

This discipline of bringing objectivity to my emotions, rather than simply giving myself over to them, has been vitally important in overcoming the destructive patterns of transference. I can work through my feelings as exactly what they are—feelings from the past—once I have objectivity about them.

I am now able to get to know people as they truly are rather than viewing them through the distorted lens of the past. My misbegotten feelings, whether positive or negative, eventually modify or drop away as my relationship with a person progresses. Growing knowledge of who the person really is replaces any distortions in my thinking, and trust develops.

I have also found that once I acknowledge that a transference is occurring, the experience can become a bridge that allows me to get in touch with otherwise inaccessible regions of my soul. The result has been a deeper experience of God's grace and transforming love.

It took me nearly eight years to understand fully what happened during the period I've just described. What I experienced was a classic example of transference related to my early relationship with my mother. We turn next to defining this phenomenon.

2
Defining Transference

The writings of British psychiatrist Dr. Frank Lake (1914–82) have helped form my understanding of transference in the context of the church. Lake worked extensively with patients suffering from mental illness related to deprivation or trauma in birth and infancy. His large teaching ministry equipped Anglican ministers to deal with these issues on a pastoral level and also helped them to find healing for deep wounds within their own souls.[1]

Shifting Perceptions

Dr. Lake concludes that transference in pastoral settings, whether in the church or other ministry situations, is unavoidable. He says, "We must not despise the inescapable human spiritual fact of transference. It arises wherever human need meets human kindliness."[2] In short, those who are effective in ministry are likely to become the objects of transference. Dr. Lake does not prescribe a remedy for this dilemma; rather he calls his readers to accept it as reality and learn how to deal with it wisely.

As a Christian and a psychiatrist he masterfully presents the relevant psychological terms needed to comprehend transference, always relating them to the Scripture. He explains not only transference but other terms, such as *repression* and *projection,* that are pertinent to his understanding of the effects of infantile trauma in adult life. For our purposes, however, I will present them here only briefly.

Transference was first defined in the early twentieth century when the first psychoanalysts, such as Sigmund Freud, noticed a pattern that emerged as they worked with their clients. Once the therapist had established trust with his client, the unresolved issues from the client's family of origin came into clearer focus as she projected them into the therapeutic relationship. As her emotions, thoughts, and memories from infancy and childhood rushed into the present, the client would misperceive her therapist, relating to him as though he was a person from the past. The therapist would then help the client understand these misperceptions, so as to gain insight into her past, resolve painful memories, and grow in her capacity to relate appropriately to others.

This phenomenon of transference has been defined more recently by the *Baker Encyclopedia of Psychology:*

> the term means literally to convey information or content from one person, place, or situation to another. The psychological usage expresses a special type of relationship with another person. The usual pattern is for a person in the present to be experienced as though he or she were a person in the past. Thus, transference, at least from a psychoanalytic point of view, is basically a repetition of an old object relationship in which attitudes and feelings, either positive or negative, pertaining to a former relationship have been shifted onto a new person in the present. Another way of describing this is to say that a mode of perceiving and responding to the world that was developed and appropriate to childhood is inappropriately transferred into the adult context.[3]

When rightly resolved, transference holds a benefit to clients. Thus some schools of psychology view it as a powerful therapeutic tool.

Burying Emotions

Repression is another widely accepted psychological term; practitioners use it to explain the internal mechanisms that keep unwanted, painful, or otherwise difficult thoughts, feelings, or memories from interfering with a person's normal range of emotions. Psychologists understand these mechanisms to be unconscious, and not things employed knowingly or intentionally. *Baker Encyclopedia of Psychology* defines repression as:

> The process by which anxiety-producing ideas or impulses are kept out of or removed from conscious awareness. It is recognized in a number of theoretical perspectives as the most basic of defense mechanisms and, according to Freud, provides the foundation on which most other defenses are constructed. Although the person is not consciously aware of repressed material or of the process of repression, this material continues to influence behavior.[4]

A certain amount of repression is seen as normal and necessary to cope with the inevitable difficulties of life. For example, a young child whose parent dies an untimely death will often learn to adopt a hopeful, expectant attitude through repressing her feelings of abandonment, uncertainty, and anxiety. The painful feelings are still there, but they lie underneath the surface of her awareness. Later in life a particular stress, such as the loss of someone dear, may cause these repressed feelings to reappear. But until then the ability to repress these emotions enables her to go on with her life.

Repression also helps us cope with the complexities of our creatureliness. Our thoughts, sensations, memories, emotions, and perceptions of reality vastly overwhelm our capacity to experience them. Because we finite creatures cannot be present to all of this at any given moment, we repress parts of our awareness so as to focus on what is immediately before us. In this sense repression is necessary for mental health.

But this mechanism can be so overdeveloped in some people that they cease to function normally. Whole facets of their humanness—their emotions, sexuality, intellectual life, and so forth—are repressed. The frustrations for such individuals, especially those whose emotions have shut down, are many. They may find it difficult to express love, or even to know when they are feeling love for another.

Or these people may be unable to express anger, even when it is appropriate and necessary. Instead they may boast of never having entertained an angry thought—when actually a colossal degree of malice is repressed in their heart.

If those suffering from repressed emotions are followers of Christ, they may find it painful to worship with others because they themselves never experience joy or gratitude in a way that inspires them to enter into worship.

The repression of emotions also hinders Christians from taking steps beyond the rudimentary basics of salvation, leaving them with a superficial spirituality. They cannot dialogue with God about matters of the deep heart because they are not in touch with them. And most significantly, they are unable to overcome sinful attitudes and reactions simply because they are unaware of them. In my experience, those who eventually transfer onto others commonly experience this excessive type of repression.

Understanding Projection

Another common feature in transferences is *projection*. Once we understand the way projection works in transference, we will see why those in transference can so gravely misperceive those on whom they are transferring.

The use of the word in psychology parallels its use in other fields. In slide photography, for example, projection refers to the technique of causing the image on the slide to be enlarged onto a blank screen through the use of light and visual lenses. Details in the photograph, though nearly invisible to the eye on the tiny slide, are displayed in crisp detail on a large screen.

In psychology, projection is defined as:

> The unconscious process by which an individual attributes to another the desires, impulses or ideas that he finds unacceptable in himself. This ego defense mechanism allows the person to take whatever is internally threatening or conflictually undesirable, whether instincts or their derivatives, and make it part of an external object or person. The conflict over the projected issue can then be dealt with as an attack from without rather than as a more ego-threatening internal struggle.[5]

In the normal course of human development, infants undergo a process of learning to distinguish their emotions from those of their parents, especially the mother. To begin with, the baby easily takes in her emotions and makes them his own. That is, the baby becomes fearful in the presence of a fearful mother, anxious when she is anxious, and so forth.

Infants also place on their mothers the responsibility for any pains they suffer, both large and small. For example, a baby may be angry with his mother if he suffers physical pain. Likewise babies look to their mothers as the source of all good and pleasurable sensations. When a mother responds to her child's emotions with understanding, reassurance, empathy, comfort, and even humor, the youngster drinks in the mother's objectivity with regard to his feelings and experiences. And her confidence that everything will turn out for the good, along with her trust in God, soaks deeply into his soul.

Even in this stage before children can speak, they begin to distinguish the difference between reality and their feelings about it, between their mother and themselves, between their feelings and their mother's feelings. Although the mother (or mother substitute) may have inadequacies, she is perceived by the child to be "good enough," as opposed to being "all good" or "all bad." When this foundation is in place, the child is prepared to form relationships with other people and to get along in the world.

Splitting, Projecting, Escaping

Just as infants project their emotions onto a "blank screen" (the mother), adults in transference project their emotions onto a person who becomes the *object* of the transference. Most commonly the object is a person, but it can be a physical article, one's own body part, an organization, or a family.

Those in transference, rather than face their painful emotions, split off from them and project them onto the object. Like infants who have difficulty distinguishing their feelings from their mother's, those in transference may mistakenly conclude that the object is experiencing the feelings that they actually have.

Frank Lake writes of the way a person in transference mistakenly attributes feelings to others:

> Every parson needs to understand and take note when a person he is helping expects him to be angry when he is not, specially devoted to a particular parishioner when he does not feel that way about her, critical when he is appreciative, impatient when he feels no impatience. It is of vital importance that he should recognize that these are only elements of the transference situation which must be fed back to the patient quite simply with some such remark as "But I don't feel like that at all. Your feelings about me come from somewhere else."[6]

This preoccupation with the emotions of others also serves to keep one's own memories and grief repressed; those in transference have no energy left to face whatever hurtful matter has surfaced in their soul. They escape the painful reality of their own suffering. Thus projection provides an illusory and temporary sense of well-being because painful emotions are cast off onto another person.[7]

Similarly, one's unacknowledged sin or evil can be projected onto the object of a transference, resulting in a false accusation. Because the object also is a flawed human being, in most instances these charges have some basis in reality. But the intensity with which they are perceived is far afield from what is real.

In transference, projection serves another purpose as well: Through it people may try to make sense of their emotions. For example, a person might project his depression onto his friend, imagining her to be depressed when she is not. He will then become preoccupied with figuring out why she is depressed. Like an amateur psychologist he may seek to uncover the reason for the depression through scrutinizing her behavior for signs of depression and probing her with questions about her childhood.

But what is actually happening in this scenario is that the person is unconsciously trying to understand his own depression by projecting it off onto his friend. The difficulty, of course, is that he will not only misperceive his friend (thereby introducing an uncomfortable sense of unreality into the friendship) but will not come any closer to understanding his own depression. Often-times those who project onto others are not readily able to distinguish their feelings from those of others, much as infants or small children are unable to distinguish their emotions from their mother's.

This dynamic becomes especially destructive when the projected emotion is a volatile one such as rageful anger or lust; it is all the more so when the object of the projection is a Christian leader. In these cases the leader's moral virtue comes under severe scrutiny. When Christians begin to accuse one another, the "accuser of the brethren" has an ideal environment in which to work, encouraging deception and a spiritual battle.

Ideal, not Real

Many transferences begin not with irrational negative feelings toward a person, but with unaccountably warm and positive sentiments. For example, in our oversexualized culture positive transferences are often the stuff of romance. Thus people often interpret their positive feelings about another to mean that they are sexually attracted to or in love with them.

A classic example of this phenomenon was featured in a psychologist's column in a local newspaper. A woman describes her feelings about her physician:

> I have a terrible problem for which I need some help. My doctor turns me on so much that I constantly think about making love to him. He is handsome, gentle, kind, and really fires me up, although he seems unaware of the effect he has on me. My husband and I are happy, but I really want to have an affair with this doctor. I wonder if I should tell the doctor about my feelings and go ahead with the affair—or would he refer me to another doctor?

The psychologist replies,

> I hope he would refer you. However, I suggest that you not share your feelings with him just yet.

Patients sometimes believe that they have fallen in love with their doctors. Or they may be irresistibly attracted to them. Although this is often considered to be normal and temporary, it is a blueprint for disaster.

A doctor's persona—the qualities he projects—is supposed to be caring, sensitive, powerful, all-knowing and unselfish.

These perceived attributes may have a profound effect on an impressionable person who is in need of a partner with these characteristics. Called "transference" in psychiatric lingo, this attraction may actually improve the therapeutic effectiveness of the doctor's treatments—up to a point.

While it is OK to idolize your doctor, the relationship must be kept on a strictly professional level. It is extremely unethical for a physician to have an affair with a patient.

If you really care about your doctor, don't tempt him or otherwise contaminate your dealings with him.

Instead, I advise you to seek counseling from an appropriate professional, such as a psychologist or a trained social worker. You need to address your sexual feelings—and not act on them.[8]

In the context of the Christian community, transferences sometimes take on a form that is identical to this woman's transference onto her doctor. For example, a woman may believe she is in love with her unmarried pastor. In these cases she may spiritualize her sexual feelings and believe that God wants them to marry. In the worst-case scenario she may pursue her minister—whether single or married—sexually. Similarly, a pastor in a transference onto his female parishioner may end up in an affair if he acts on his sexual feelings.

More commonly, however, positive transferences take the form of an idealized view of another person that does not have overtly sexual overtones. Although this may seem less volatile, it can be harder to detect, especially in a church setting.

Scott's Story

An example of this kind of idealization, which almost always catches a member of the clergy by surprise, follows in Scott's story.[9]

Growing Up, Breaking Free

Scott came from a family who didn't attend church. His father, a military man, was both distant from and critical of his son. His mother did her best to compensate for her husband's frequent and extended absences—both actual and emotional—from the home. But she found it extremely difficult to cope with this challenging parenting situation and was often demonstratively angry and frustrated.

As the oldest child, Scott felt responsible not only to help his mom with the younger children but to ease her loneliness and soothe her frazzled emotions. As he entered his teen years he had little time or energy for interests or friends outside his home. And when it was time for college he enrolled at a local university in order to be near enough to continue helping his mother.

During his college years Scott became a Christian and was nurtured in his new faith through a ministry on campus. As he matured as a Christian he realized that he needed to make a healthy break from his family. With this in mind, and despite his fear about what would happen to his mother, he took a teaching job in a city several hundred miles away from his parents' home.

An Idealized Perception

For several months Scott struggled to find a local church. Eventually he settled on one whose pastor was warm, fatherly, and intent on helping his parishioners find places to serve. Initially Scott perceived the pastor as being the most loving, dynamic, Christ-like man he had ever met. Confident that he had found an uncommonly good pastor, Scott began to pour his youthful energy into the life of the church.

The new member eagerly anticipated every interaction with his pastor, freely expressing to him his admiration and gratitude. Scott felt an unusual closeness with him; something he longed for but rarely experienced with his own father. These feelings were based partly on the warm relationship he had with the pastor and partly on the pastor's truly good, Christ-like qualities.

But Scott's perception of the pastor also grew out of the deprivations of his childhood. Because of these, he held an idealized image of what he desired in a father-figure. The pastor had no way of knowing this, of course, and responded to Scott's enthusiasm by extending friendship to him and encouraging him to take an active role in the youth ministry of the church.

After about two years Scott went through an unusual time of stress at the school where he was teaching because of a change in the administration. He also began to experience some depression and generalized feelings of insecurity and anxiety. Unknown to him, the uncertainty of his work situation was driving to the surface the unresolved issues with his father.

From Positive to Negative

Scott's intense, childish need for father-love and affirmation had intensified in his stressful circumstance and was now directed toward his pastor. He began to ask outright for more of his time and attention, both personally and in relation to his service in the church. At other times he used subtle manipulation to get his needs met.

At first the pastor believed he should give Scott some extra attention as a way of supporting him through the difficult work situation. He assumed the relationship would return to normal once Scott's stress lessened. But even as the situation at the school began to settle down, Scott's demands on the pastor continued to intensify.

On a few occasions the minister's growing frustration and impatience with Scott became apparent in their conversations. To the pastor's dismay, Scott was shocked and hurt to observe these emotions. The man in transference could not accept his minister's normal, human emotions because his idealized image left no room for them.

The pastor finally began to set appropriate boundaries in his relationship with Scott. And, in a predictable fashion, Scott interpreted these measures as a personal rejection and began to project all of his bitterness toward his father onto the pastor. At this point the transference was no longer positive, but negative.

A Challenge and a Response

The pastor, realizing the need for action, secured the help of a trusted person and confronted Scott. Scott responded well to their challenge and sought professional counseling. Over the course of the next two years Scott's relationship with his pastor was understandably strained and awkward. But slowly, as Scott worked through his transference and as the pastor held fast to the personal boundaries that he had set, the relationship was repaired and actually grew stronger.

A minister could easily become wary of all praise and affirmation after a few experiences with people like Scott. But all parishioners are not like Scott; some are good judges of character who can truly admire praiseworthy qualities in pastors or leaders and love them for it. When in doubt, we learn to ask the Lord for discernment to distinguish true expressions of praise, appreciation, and gratitude from dangerous idealizations.

Educating the Emotions

As we have seen and will continue to see, cases of transference can usually be traced back to childhood. One reason for this relates to the way a child's appropriate emotional development depends in large part upon the help parents give by way of example and instruction.

Another reason concerns the child's ability to repress his thoughts and feelings in a proper way, which also depends largely on the parents. They are needed to help him understand his emotions, and especially those that arise in response to real suffering or deprivation. When parents lack this capacity to "educate" their child's emotions lovingly and wisely (or when some physical or psychological injury blocks the ability to receive this help), the child will bog down in emotional immaturity.

Of course the parents' ability to help children rightly manage emotions depends upon the parenting they themselves have received. If inadequate, they in turn fail to educate their children's emotions, with serious consequences. Some of these children learn to repress their memories and feelings to such an extent that they never understand the mysterious forces in their souls. Instead they seem to exist in a realm of superficial externals, largely devoid of depth. They are hindered from feeling deeply about the most important things in their lives.

Other children are given license by their parents' example to give full vent to their feelings. These children and the people around them suffer under the tyranny of these unwieldy emotions. In the worst cases, some of these individuals become delinquents and later criminals.

Still other children, those of more prosperous and well-educated homes, are often schooled in the way of sentimentalism. They learn to be guided by their feelings to the neglect of reason and moral effort, thus becoming stunted in their capacity to engage creatively with the painful realities of life. Such people are emotionally immature, whether they fall into the extreme of repressing all emotion or living by the dictates of their feelings.

Thankfully Christians are never bound and limited by any deficiencies in the parenting they may have received. As we will see in examples in the coming chapters, even the most deprived people can receive the needed wisdom if they petition God to send them help.[10]

3

Replayed Memories

*W*hen repressed memories begin to surface, as they do in transference, past experiences and feelings are often superimposed onto present relationships. When this happens those in transference unconsciously set up a scenario that resembles an event from the past; they then attempt to replay the painful memories in the hope for a more satisfying resolution. The classic example is a daughter of an alcoholic who, against her former vows, marries an alcoholic. She hopes her husband will change, and love her as her father never could.

Sigmund Freud and his colleagues were keenly aware of this dynamic as it appeared in their cases; they understood it to be an integral part of transference. Freud wrote, "We soon perceive that the transference is itself only a piece of repetition, and that the repetition is a transference of the forgotten past not only onto the doctor but also onto all the other aspects of the current situation."[1]

Freud called this the "repetition compulsion." He saw it as a way that people tried to recall important—and unresolved—memories from their past that they were loath to remember. He explained, "The patient does not remember anything of what he has forgotten and repressed, but acts it out. He reproduces it not as a memory but as an action; he repeats it without, of course, knowing he is repeating it at all."[2]

The need to revisit hurtful memories and past family dynamics occurs even in early childhood and sheds light on the role of replayed memories in adult transferences. If parents understand this phenomenon they can help their children work through memories; the youngsters can then reach a place of resolution before they leave childhood.

Trauma at Birth

Mark and Gigi are an example of parents who grappled with the dynamic of replayed memories. They were able to help their son, Mark David, work through his emotional reactions to an early traumatic experience.

When Gigi was pregnant with Mark David she began labor completely exhausted. Having endured a gall-bladder operation in her third month and constant nausea throughout the pregnancy, she literally lacked the strength to deliver the baby. She received a high level of pitocin to induce labor. Several hours later Gigi complained of excruciating pain, and the doctors decided that they needed to perform a cesarean section.

With three other women also in emergency situations waiting for the same procedure, Gigi was told she was fourth in line. She suffered for two hours without any pain reliever because of the risk to the baby. When she was finally brought to the operating room and given a spinal anesthetic, her body was so stressed that her jaw was locked shut.

Once the incision was made, the surgeon had to remove the baby with forceps because the head had become wedged in the birth canal. Later Gigi said that when at last the baby was brought to her, she did not want to see him and greeted him only out of a sense of obligation. Twelve hours later, however, she was more rested and enjoyed a special time alone with little Mark David.

Although mother and child recovered physically from the birth, both were emotionally traumatized. Gigi admitted to feeling angry and resentful toward the child, even though she knew better rationally. She began to pray earnestly about her emotional response to her newborn son.

Playing Baby-in-the-Tummy

To all appearances, Mark David was a placid infant. But as he grew and began to express his emotions, his parents became aware that he had a problem with inordinate anger. Any emotion aroused in him, whether surprise, excitement, delight, pleasure, or sadness, eventually turned into anger. Long before the terrible twos, Mark David threw fits of rage when he did not get his way.

Mark and Gigi, at a loss as to how to help their son, sought counsel from mature Christians. They were advised to pray for the child each night after he had fallen asleep, asking the Holy Spirit to descend into whatever was amiss, including memories of the trauma at birth.

They were faithful to pray for Mark David for many months. They were also careful to put loving and consistent boundaries around his behavior when he expressed anger, thereby teaching him what was appropriate and what would not be tolerated. He seemed to learn slowly, however, and they continued to cry out to God for a breakthrough.

When Mark David was about three years old, Gigi was astonished one day when he asked her, "Can we play baby-in-the-tummy?" He told her precisely how the game was to be played: She was to lie down on her back and he would lie beside her, near her abdomen. On the floor next to them he laid his pacifier and a few toys and instructed her to give him these gifts when he was born. Finally he covered himself with his baby blanket and gave her further instructions: "Say hello to the baby, Mommy. Tell him you can feel him moving now."

After several minutes of this kind of dialogue, Mark David would throw off the blanket and stand on his feet, scrunch up his face, and say, "Ma-ma, ma-ma." In response Gigi exclaimed how glad she was to see him, while holding him close.

Mark David asked to play this game every night for about three months, and occasionally thereafter. Gigi was patient and prayed for the Lord's strength to "greet the baby" even when she was exhausted. Slowly the child's overwhelming anger subsided and gave way to a sense of well-being.

Under the Blaze of Love

Two years later another critical moment occurred in the shaping of Mark David's emotions when Gigi was two months away from giving birth. Mark David took a keen interest in the process of her pregnancy, especially wondering how the baby would get out of his mother's stomach. He asked more frequently to play the "baby-in-the-tummy" game.

One day while playing the game he interrupted his usual script and asked his mother, "Did it hurt you when I was born?" When she explained that it did indeed, the boy's face turned white and he said, quietly and fearfully, "I'm sorry, Mommy."

Gigi told him that her suffering was not his fault because sometimes such things happen in an imperfect world. She assured him that his birth was well worth any pain she had suffered and that she was truly glad he was born. Upon hearing these reassuring words the color returned to his face and he burst into tears. Mark David fell into his mother's arms, receiving her love precisely where he had experienced its absence at birth.

Gigi had an extraordinary capacity to enter into her son's world of play and to communicate her joy in his birth through her prayers, words, and touch. She had the patience to reassure him again and again of her love until he truly believed it. As she educated his emotions, his fears and anger shrank down to normal size.

In the steady blaze of his parents' love and wisdom, the anger that once dominated Mark David's soul—causing every emotional experience to mutate into rage—came to be rightly related to his other emotions and to the people around him. He gained not only control over his feelings but also the capacity to empathize with another's pain (in this case his mother's), seeing his own suffering in a new light.

This story also illustrates the way the soul replays painful scenarios from birth through childhood, each time seeking a better outcome. As we will see below, this can extend into adulthood as these scripts interweave with new circumstances while past memories are projected into the present.

Ambivalence, Fears, Faith

An example of the way unresolved memories from childhood can relate to transference in adulthood is my own experience some nine years after my transference onto Cindy.

I had received a great deal of insight and prayer for healing in the years between these two experiences, but one key memory remained unresolved. When dealt with, I was able to overcome my anger toward my mother and fully accept myself as a woman. The memory was triggered when I bought an infant baptismal gown while helping to conduct a Pastoral Care Ministry school led by Leanne Payne in Belgium. For me this purchase held tremendous symbolic significance. At the time I had been married for about seven years, and my husband and I had been trying to conceive a child for about a year.

For some time I had been aware of my ambivalence about having children. On the one hand, I was ready to welcome a child into the circle of love that had grown strong between Mark and me. But on the other, my enthusiasm was dampened by lingering fears: Given the deprivation of my early years, would I be able to nurture a child adequately? Would I end up passing on to my children the same wounds that my grandmother passed on to my mother, and my mother to me?

I was also ambivalent about becoming pregnant, as was clear by my lack of grief and disappointment at the beginning of my menstrual cycles. Unlike other women who were trying to conceive, I felt relieved. As I prayed about my feelings, I realized that the reluctance to have children indicated that I had not yet accepted this aspect of my femininity. I began to ask the Lord to awaken this desire in my heart.

I had been praying about my feelings for several months when we arrived in the medieval city of Bruges for a few days of rest before the start of a week of ministry. In one of their famous lace shops I beheld a beautiful baptismal gown and instantly wanted to buy it. Right away, I knew this desire had been planted in my heart by the Holy Spirit in answer to my prayers. To purchase the gown symbolized my desire to bring children into the world, and to baptize them into the family of God.

All the while, however, my ambivalence about having children was still very much alive. So I bought the gown in faith, despite my lingering fears. In doing this I unexpectedly accessed inexplicable but deep emotions, so strong in fact that I immediately began to dissociate. I began to lose my ability to stay in tune with my present surroundings.

While I was yet in the shop paying for the gown I began to experience some peculiar symptoms common to dissociation: I felt disoriented in terms of direction and time[3] and my field of vision seemed altered. Also, my body suddenly felt tense, especially in my jaws and face. Finally, I felt unusually self-conscious—like a shy child among adults—when later I joined my friends for lunch.

Feelings of Unreality

After lunch I walked back to our hotel with Leanne. We initiated my new, delicate, Belgian-made teacups and enjoyed a meaningful conversation over tea, sparked by the baptismal gown and all that was awakening in my heart. Before leaving her room we made special plans for dinner. Both of us wanted to eat early and avoid the crowded, smoke-filled restaurant where the rest of the team would gather. All the while I continued to feel very disoriented, but said nothing to her. I told her that I would be resting in my room for the afternoon, and we agreed on a time to meet in the early evening.

But once in my room I found myself unusually restless and decided to take a walk. For some reason it never occurred to me to inform Leanne of my change of plans. After I left my room, my feelings of unreality grew stronger and I worried about getting lost. I was also frustrated about being ridiculously indecisive over making small purchases in the shops lining the streets, something uncharacteristic of me.

Eventually I met up with other members of the ministry team and their company helped me to feel more anchored in reality.

But my connection with what was going on around me was only partial: It was as though I had one foot in the present reality of Bruges, Belgium, and the other one in some different place and time. The plans I had made earlier with Leanne became lost to me. Through my dissociation I had come up with some other plan of which she knew nothing.

In the meantime, Leanne had been trying to reach me by phone. Soon two hours had passed since our agreed meeting time and she became extremely worried. When she had concluded that I was missing, no one was available to tell her of my whereabouts; the entire ministry team was out of reach. In desperation, she set out after nightfall to look for me.

Yanked Back to Reality

In retrospect, Leanne's discovery of me in an Italian restaurant with the rest of the ministry team was remarkably funny. For one thing, we were the only group of Americans. And when Leanne walked in she was bundled up against the cold February winds with a wide-rimmed black hat, a long black coat, gloves, and fogged-up glasses. Upon seeing me she cried out, "Valerie, where have you been!?" Conversations stopped all around the room and everyone looked at us. We held their attention only for a moment, however. They were not surprised at such behavior from American tourists.

My experience of those few moments was most unusual; after hearing Leanne's first sentence, I could hear nothing more. I could only see her lips moving and her arms waving in exclamation. I felt cocooned in a silent, private world, completely separated from my surroundings. Yet in that solitary place I was keenly aware that God was with me, speaking to me.

I heard his instructions very plainly: he wanted me to put my trust in him and stay connected with him—and with Leanne. With all the strength of my will I chose to obey the Lord's word to me at that moment. Instantly I was able to tune back into reality and to mutter a confused apology to Leanne.

Behind Leanne's outburst of concern lay her utter astonishment over such an unlikely end to that particular afternoon. My behavior was inexplicable for two reasons. First, in the three years in which we had worked closely together, I had proven to be reliable; she had no reason to expect anything different on this day.

Second, we had enjoyed an especially delightful time of conversation that afternoon. I left her in the warm glow of our interaction with the anticipation that we would have an equally satisfactory meal together that evening. Leanne had no reason to suspect that I would completely disappear in just a few hours time.

Somehow her strong emotional response and my decision to align my will with God's yanked me back into reality. Except for the extreme tension in my body, all my other symptoms of dissociation disappeared.

The Real Battle

Before I returned to the hotel that night I took a long walk with other members of the team. I became aware of their concern for me and their shock at Leanne's outburst. I could have easily galvanized their sympathy for me, against Leanne. But nothing could have been more destructive, I realized, and I chose to say nothing.

That night I had a dream that warned me of the spiritual battle surrounding the situation. In the dream I was in a shop in Bruges with Leanne and Mario Bergner, an important member of the team. Into the store walked a woman who, a few years back, brought a diabolical disunity to the team when Mario was struggling through his transference onto Leanne. The woman tried to draw me away from Leanne and Mario and into conversation with herself.

I awakened knowing that the woman symbolized the way the Evil One was at work to bring disunity to the team. And I realized that I, in particular, was being targeted because of my vulnerabilities.

In a flash I could see the whole picture: I was in danger of becoming stuck in my healing process and forfeiting not only all I had gained but the ministry God had given me. I also realized that the battle was directed as forcefully against Leanne and her ministry as it was against me.

Leanne, in fact, was battle-weary over the loss of several she deeply loved due to unresolved transferences; I could easily become one more to add to the list. Also at risk was the effectiveness of the mission for which God had called us to Belgium. Through God's gift of my discerning the spiritual battle, I was motivated to cry out for protection and a way through this difficulty.

Soon I became plagued by a deluge of painful thoughts and feelings, although as yet I had no sense of their origin. At the foremost I dealt with emotions of anger and fear. My mind was preoccupied with fantasies of abandonment—both of being abandoned by Leanne and my leaving her. For example, I imagined that I had become such a problem to Leanne and the team that I would have to separate from them.

Alternatively, I thought I would like to pack my bags, take a cab to the airport, and fly home. The sure knowledge that this was precisely the wrong action kept me from acting on my impulses: I knew my feelings were irrational, born out of my transference of feelings from the past into the present.

Release and Healing

Several days into the conference, the intensity of my misery reached a peak and I withdrew to my room as the evening session began. Knowing full well that my intense anger was only symbolically related to Leanne, I was desperate to find relief from it. I feared that it would explode in a sinful way against her.

As I pleaded with God to help me, I was given a vivid seeing of Christ crucified for me, of his dying to take into himself my sinful, angry reaction. Finally a release of tears came, and I was able to come present to and let go of the anger that was burning so furiously in my soul.

I then made my way to the evening session, determined not to minister to anyone but instead to hide at the edges of the meeting room. Leanne was in the middle of her lecture on a child's need for a sense of well-being when I arrived and found a seat next to an elderly Belgian man.

As the prayer time began, this gentleman turned to me with tears in his eyes and asked me to pray for him. Out of pity I tentatively laid my hands on him and began to pray. To my surprise and delight, the Holy Spirit began to minister deeply to him—and to me. I realized then that my healing would continue even as I prayed for others.

Just as the session was ending, a young mother with her baby boy came to my attention. I asked her permission, and then prayed as I gently made the sign of the cross on the boy's forehead. In response, the little one wiggled and laughed for joy. His giggles were infectious, touching me and his mother deeply.

I slept soundly that night, after five nights of sleeplessness. And when I awakened the next morning I was keenly aware that I was once again back to normal. At this point I knew that I was objective enough to talk with Leanne about the incident in the restaurant, and to make a more heartfelt apology for causing her such anxiety.

She extended her forgiveness to me, and likewise asked my forgiveness for expressing her concern so forcefully in public. She explained how stunned she had been by my behavior. Suggesting that perhaps I had dissociated, she wondered if this was behind the misunderstanding about where and when we were to meet for dinner. Remembering the strange symptoms I had experienced, I was more than ready to concur with her assessment of the situation. The reason for the dissociation, however, was yet unclear to us.

Several days later we returned to the United States. As I asked the Lord for insight, a root memory came up that was related to the suppressed thoughts and feelings about my mother. It had always been one of my most vivid childhood memories, one I could remember at will, but always without any feeling. We turn to the experience and its significance next.

4

Childhood Roots

One day when I was four and Tracy, my friend and neighbor, was five, we decided it was time for a tea party. We put on our best dresses and knocked on the door of Mrs. Boyd, a grandmotherly lady who lived next to my parents. She invited us into her front room and served us cookies and tea from lovely china. We talked endlessly—about what I cannot remember.

Twice during our tea party Tracy's older sister knocked on the screen door, telling me that I should go home because my mother was looking for me. Both times I ignored her. I was only too ready to believe Tracy, who assured me that her sister was making up these warnings to ruin our tea party.

I can still vividly remember how the light of the setting sun streamed into the room when we finally left Mrs. Boyd's house. It had turned to early evening, and I had been missed at the dinner table. When I appeared in my front yard, my mother stormed out of the house, beside herself with worry. I had been a compliant child and had never before caused her such anxiety. She scolded me and promptly gave me the first—and only—spanking I ever received.

In reaction I ran straight to my room, closed the curtains, jumped into bed, and yanked the covers over my head. My mother knocked at the door and told me to come to dinner, but I did not respond. Finally my father came into the room and sat on my bed. I steadfastly remained buried under the covers while he explained that he and my mother were not angry with me but had been terribly worried.

He did everything he could to persuade me to emerge from under the covers and come to dinner. I told him I was not hungry—which was undoubtedly true, given the number of cookies I had eaten with my tea. I remained intensely angry with my mother, even hating her. Pitying myself, I felt she had treated me unfairly and shamed me. I stayed in my room all night.

My mother and I both remember a change in the way I related to my parents after that experience; thereafter I preferred my father's company over my mother's. It was more than ten years later, when I was converted to the Christian faith, before I began to identify strongly with my mother again. Until then my childhood was characterized by discomfort and fear when in the presence of other girls and women, including my mother.

By contrast, I found it easy to interact with boys and men, especially my father. His world of invention and creation captured my imagination, and I have many wonderful memories of sitting beside him at his workbench, watching him build and fix things. I deeply identified with him, evidenced in my boyish way of dress and my masculinized dreams of what I would be when I grew up.

The Real Memory

While praying about my experience in Bruges, the memory of the tea party came back to me very strongly. Unlike my previous recollections, however, this time I remembered clearly the thoughts and emotions I had felt as a four-year-old. Taking the form of a monologue to my mother, the tirade was full of revenge, resentment, spite, anger, and self-pity. In addition, it was replete with the sort of expletives my father used when he was angry. It was much like my mutterings under the covers that day after my mother had spanked me.

In writing out this monologue I felt ashamed and embarrassed that such feelings were still lurking in my soul. It was difficult, but I painstakingly put down all the diseased thoughts and feelings about my mother that had been repressed for twenty-seven years. After this exercise I was able to forgive her fully, at a deep level.

Upon reflection I saw how as a four-year-old I had fully rejected both my mother and, thus, my own femininity. Underlying this repudiation was my failure as an infant to bond adequately with her and the intense infantile rage that had resulted. My disappearance as a little girl was not as innocent as it appeared, but was an expression of my anger and malice toward my mother.

Later in Bruges, as I pressed through my fears to buy the baptismal gown, I came present to this same anger. Because it was so intense and potentially disabling, I immediately tried to repress it by dissociating from the whole situation—including my appointment with Leanne. At the same time, as the repressed anger toward my mother surfaced, I initially, and unknowingly, transferred it onto Leanne. These two powerful factors influenced my disappearance in Bruges that afternoon.

Rewriting the Script

I later understood how my relationship with Leanne became the stage, so to speak, on which I attempted to reenact—however unconsciously—this childhood memory in the hope for a better outcome. My disappearance from Leanne in Belgium had a striking resemblance to my disappearance from my mother as a four-year-old.

The part of the script that needed rewriting was my own, not my mother's or Leanne's. As a child I had irrationally rejected my mother and all the trappings of little-girlness over a minor case of embarrassment because she scolded and spanked me; punishment I most certainly deserved. This memory was replayed in my disappearance in Bruges, and consequently in Leanne's reprimand in the restaurant.

My temptation in the restaurant was to exaggerate the significance of Leanne's reaction and use it to justify rejecting her, much as I had once rejected my mother. To do this would have been to choose to remain in the childish and even infantile reaction to my mother.

But instead of transferring my anger toward my mother onto Leanne, with God's help I chose to face it. Then I was able to resolve the issue before God by forgiving the person who had actually hurt me, my mother. I also chose to trust Leanne, thereby resisting the temptation to reject her. In doing this I effectively rewrote the script of my earlier rejection of woman and all things feminine.

The end of the story is a happy one: Mark and I conceived our first child about two weeks after my return from Belgium.

Taking It to the Cross

Prayer was essential in this process of understanding my experience in Bruges. When kneeling in prayer I would feel the Holy Spirit come to me as Comforter and Helper. There, in the strong and gentle safety of God's presence, I could press through my defenses and allow my repressed emotions to arise.

While I was in this responsive posture before God, the comfort of the Holy Spirit was poured into the places in my heart where I still felt the hurt of a little girl who longed for a greater connection with her mother. Along with this much-needed solace came the illuminating light of Christ that enabled me to understand the sinful ways I had reacted toward my mother and other women throughout my life. And in this same light I could then understand how my behavior in Bruges was related to the memory from my childhood.

When other painful thoughts and feelings have arisen from infantile injuries, I have learned what to do with them. Two disciplines in particular have been the most useful. The one described above is keeping a prayer journal where I can write out my confused thinking before God.

The other discipline is using a crucifix in prayer. The results have been dramatic when, in the midst of suffering, I look at or hold on to a crucifix and release my pain onto Christ crucified. Not only has this facilitated my healing, but it has averted other potential transferences by bringing me back to the sure knowledge of the origin of my suffering and the only remedy—the full resolution of my pain at the cross.

Frank Lake writes of the help to be found for the sufferer in the solace of identifying with Jesus in his suffering:

> The Spirit of Christ . . . did bear all the extremities of persecution and affliction. That is what His Cross and Passion assure us of. He carried this unique experience of patient endurance of human suffering, through death, into the risen life God gave him. The very same Spirit of Christ "descended" on the Church at Pentecost and has been with us and in us as Christians ever since. It is this Spirit of God, able to endure all things with the fortitude of the Son, who has sustained the martyrs and upheld the afflicted. He is our first and final resource, when, in clinical pastoral care, we encourage Christians who seriously "want to get to the bottom of their trouble" to turn and face the emergence of whatever threatens the self from within. The divine gift of fortitude has been made available to us at great cost to the donor.[1]

Living with a Miracle

Understanding the significance of my infantile relationship to my mother has been key in making sense of my transference onto Cindy and my experience in Belgium. Behind that relationship, of course, is my mother's own early personal history.

For the first five years of her life my mother was separated from her own mother. She lived on a tiny farm on Blue Mesa in western Colorado with her maternal grandparents; they were very poor and barely eked out a living. They loved her dearly but could not be the kind of mother-substitute my mom needed in infancy. Ever since, she has suffered under the shadow of a painful sense of rejection by her father and abandonment by her mother.

I was born when my mother was thirty. She and my father had been trying to have children for ten years and were thrilled when they discovered Mom was pregnant. Even though they were not Christians, they called me their miracle baby.

The joy, however, dissipated when I was born. My mother was extremely anxious about me as an infant; she was afraid to pick me up for fear of dropping me and was overwhelmed by the many details of my care. Lacking a sense of well-being, she was unable to impart one to me.

When I was a year old Mom went back to work. Later she told me that she didn't do so for financial reasons, but because she was afraid she would lose her mind if she continued to stay at home alone with me. My very first memory is of waking up in the bedroom of my baby-sitter's home, crying for my mother and anxiously pressing against my genitals with a blanket.

I received my first glimpse of insight into this painful, guilt-ridden memory when after college I attended a lecture by Leanne Payne at a Pastoral Care Ministry school. She explained that anxiety and dread are experienced by the infant as a sensation of uncomfortable tension in the genital area:

> The infant, unable to receive the love of the mother or someone other than himself, will anxiously clutch at his own genitals. . . . This is the pain and dread of being *dis-related*, first of all as an infant to its mother. In this separation, the infant can fail to achieve a sense of well-being or even of being at all.[2]

The Skeletons in My Room

A recurring dream from my early childhood gives a vivid picture of the depth of anxiety and dread I experienced as a baby. In the dream I would see two rocking chairs, one full-size and the other a child-size miniature. I would look first at the child's chair and see seated in it a white, child-size skeleton. Then I would turn to look at the big chair. Seated there would be another skeleton, this one of an adult. I would wake from these dreams in sheer terror.

The rocking chairs I saw in my dream were actual pieces of furniture in my room. I was so disturbed by them that eventually I gave the little chair to my younger brother to put in his room. When he asked why I didn't want it, I told him about the dreams. Fearing they might have something to do with the chair, we decided to take it to the basement, where it remained until my parents gave it away.

The adult skeleton symbolizes how I experienced my mother—as lifeless, brittle, and having nothing to give. And the tiny skeleton depicts how deeply I identified with her lifelessness. My view of woman was drastically affected, both in terms of what I could receive from other women and what I believed I was capable of giving.

I need to underline that on the surface my daily relations with my mother throughout my childhood and adolescence were harmonious. Especially in my teenage years, the good relationship I had with my mom was the envy of many of my peers who were in open conflict with their mothers. I was able to make the best of my relationship with my mother by repressing the pain of my early experience.

I also split off from my emotional reactions. Had I not repressed my strong feelings of rage, hatred, anxiety, dread, fear, self-pity, and resentment, they would have been a barrier to relating to my mother. Therefore I placed my emotions in a sealed-off room in my soul, so to speak, to keep them from overwhelming the rest of my life.

Although this mechanism of splitting allowed me to function better in my family, my whole capacity to feel was dulled. I lacked the ability to respond emotionally to people and situations, even when I wanted or needed to.

Erupting Emotions

Occasionally during childhood my painful emotions erupted into the present. When this happened I was overwhelmed with feelings that I did not understand and could not control, such as a deep sense of hatred and dread toward particular women in my life. The most memorable example occurred with my second-grade reading teacher.

That year I had experienced some unusual changes. My homeroom teacher, whom I was very fond of, took a special interest in me and initiated a series of tests to determine whether my placement in her class for slower readers had been mistaken. Based on the results, it was decided that I should leave the classroom of my beloved teacher during the reading period and go to the class for more advanced readers.

I took an instant dislike to Mrs. Johnson, my new reading teacher. I have memories of her kindly pleading with me to please smile, but I refused not only to smile but to speak to her. Even when I was called upon to answer questions, I would not. This marked the beginning of four years of rarely talking in school. My behavior was so troubling to the teachers that they discussed the matter with my mother. She was bewildered by their concern and could only tell them that I seemed to talk normally at home and among my neighborhood friends.

My last memory of Mrs. Johnson dates several years later. One day when I was in sixth grade, she was the substitute teacher for my gym class. Upon seeing her and realizing that she was the dreaded Mrs. Johnson from second grade, I was overwhelmed with feelings of hatred and anxiety and began to weep uncontrollably. I cried for several hours and, when asked why I was crying, could give no explanation.

Such unexpected eruptions of repressed emotions were precursors of my transference onto Cindy. Later I learned that these perplexing experiences throughout my childhood and in my relationship with Cindy were not unique. Frank Lake comments on this extremely common reaction to infantile suffering:

> The roots of all the psychoneuroses lie in infantile experiences of mental pain of such an intolerable severity as to require splitting off from consciousness at about the time that they occurred. These have remained buried by repression. The actual cause of the panic may be a time of separation-anxiety endured during the early months of life, when to be separated from the sight and sensory perception of the source of "being," in mother or her substitute, is tantamount to a slow strangling of the spirit and its impending death.[3]

I have seen this dynamic replayed repeatedly in the lives of other people, especially those in the church and other ministry settings. Most of the time, those involved are not equipped to understand what is happening, much less resolve the problem.

The dynamic of transference can be overlooked or misdiagnosed even by those who have received psychological training. The reason is simple: Transference is understood too narrowly as something that occurs only in the confines of a therapist's professional practice.

Roots outside Infancy

Although difficulty in the dynamic of the infant-mother relationship underlies many transferences, and is almost always at the root of the most confusing and distorted, not all transferences have their genesis in infancy. Many involve the effects of broken relationships and painful experiences from later in childhood and after.

One example is Marty's story, whose transferences as an adult were related to his experiences during the school-age years. When Marty was five, his mother died unexpectedly. He cannot remember many details about her, but he has treasured photographs of himself as a small child with his mother.

From the accounts of those who knew her well, Marty's mother was an especially strong Christian and an exemplary wife and mother. When she died she left four children and their father to go on with life without her. This, of course, seemed impossible to all of them, but especially to Marty's father.

Not long after her death, Marty remembers terrible changes happening in his father. Being utterly overwhelmed with the practical responsibilities of parenting four children by himself, his dad married again in desperation. In the children's estimation, his new wife was an especially poor replacement for their beloved mother. Their resentment of her only added to the tension in their home.

Marty cannot remember exactly when it began, but his father began disciplining the children unmercifully. Worst of all, he instituted a ritual of beating the two boys upon his return from the Sunday evening church service. Marty's stepmother, herself fearful of her husband's violence, did nothing to protect the children.

To escape the tension at home Marty enlisted in the army during the Korean War, volunteering for active duty. After a short time in battle he was discharged with a full mental breakdown. He bounced back quickly, however, marrying and embarking on a highly successful career. And in contrast to his father's hypocrisy, Marty was consistent in his service in the church and his home life.

Marty had buried the pain of his childhood under the image of his success; his frantic workaholism left no time for reflection on the past. But eventually he began to display symptoms of the most severe form of suicidal depression.

With great determination, and despite extreme setbacks, he found the medical help he needed to manage his depression. The pain of his childhood, however, remained largely unresolved. When asked if he felt anger toward his father, Marty replied, "No, I don't feel anything in regard to my father. I don't feel love, I don't feel hate. I feel nothing." Clearly, his feelings were repressed.

Although buried, the angry emotions were still lurking in Marty's soul. Sometime after his depression was stabilized, a situation arose in which Marty transferred them onto the assistant pastor in his church.

Marty had become aware of a difficulty in a relationship between this minister and a parishioner. After listening to the story Marty became suspicious of the pastor, whom he had hitherto trusted and admired. Marty felt compelled to take up the parishioner's case, and over a course of several months he talked to a number of people who were disgruntled with the pastor.

He eventually came to the conclusion that the pastor had an inordinate problem with anger and felt compelled to make sure that this problem was addressed and corrected. He became obsessed with making his case against the pastor. Sadly, the situation was not resolved and eventually both the pastor and Marty left the church.

Projection and Misperception

Marty's story is an example of transference having roots in relationships later in childhood. The emotions that issued out of the overwhelming loss of his mother, coupled with his father's physical abuse, were the stuff of his transference onto the pastor. The typical features of transference are prominent throughout his story.

First was the projection of Marty's anger onto the pastor. Although the minister had expressed anger in several frustrating situations, his emotions were not so out of control as to disqualify him from ministry, as Marty believed. Rather, Marty projected his own repressed anger onto the pastor—effectively making a mountain out of a molehill. This was Marty's way of evading the realization that his childhood anger still raged within him.

Second was the misperception of a person in the present based on Marty's relationship with his father. Marty misperceived the pastor as being like his father and set out to prove that he was as hypocritical as his father had been.

Finally was a pattern of trying to reconstruct and resolve the abusive scenario of his childhood through a situation in the present. Marty cast the pastor in the part of an abuser and then attempted to exact a confession and apology from him. Although he desperately desired this from his father, he never received it. He became an advocate for those who had been "abused" by the pastor even as he had so desperately needed someone to protect and rescue him as a child.

We have explored the roots of repression through incidents in infancy and childhood. What happens to the repressed emotions? Why do they start coming up? What keeps them from surfacing? And where can we find healing and resolution from the pain of the past? It is to these issues that we turn next.

5

Repression, Pride, and Self-Deception

hy does the buried stuff of the heart sometimes burst back up? The answers to this
question are varied and may seem contradic-
tory. Three in particular stand out.

For some people one reason is unusual stress. Most often this
factor affects those who normally order their lives well and who
thrive in a structured environment. At times their organization
can be turned topsy-turvy by major life changes such as marriage, the birth of a baby, a job change, moving house, serious illness, the death of someone close, retirement, aging, and so forth.
What often results are unresolved events of the past, long repressed, reasserting themselves.

Commenting on this, Frank Lake writes,

> Affliction needs no uncovering in certain unfortunate people. It
> is overt with its burden of psychic wretchedness. In others—I
> think of many clergy of whom this is true—it lies for the most part
> below the surface of consciousness. . . . Here the fuller uncover-

ing of the dark side [repressed emotions] may be touched off by a variety of physical, emotional and spiritual changes. Exhausting illness or excessive fatigue; retirement or aging; maturation or resistance to normal development; spiritual disobedience or profound and painful obedience; all these may provoke the upthrust of ancient injuries, and give to the astonished ego the opportunity to be reunited to long-alienated elements of its total selfhood.[1]

A second reason is precisely the opposite from the first: For some people a lack of stress can lead to the breakdown of their powers of repression. These people thrive on action, a full schedule, and responsibility; in extreme cases, they prefer pandemonium to predictability.

In contrast to those who love order and solitude, these people dread structure and being alone. In such times they often experience depression, anxiety, anger, and so forth; ironically, a period of unusual security and safety can cause them to become undone. For such people only the safe environment of a loving Christian community, especially tight-knit fellowship with a few trusted friends, will free them to let down their defenses and allow the repressed matter to come up.

Apart from the factor of unusual stress or the lack thereof, I have observed a third common reason for the failure of repression—the formation of an emotionally dependent relationship. Such a relationship can be described as one in which two people have between them inadequate or inappropriate emotional, intellectual, spiritual, or physical boundaries. Such friendships are characterized by attitudes of exclusivity, jealousy, and emotional volatility on the part of one or both parties.

In such relationships, one person (or both) quite often regresses into an immature way of relating, usually to precisely that time in their life in which issues were left unresolved. For example, in my relationship with Cindy, I regressed into a way of relating that would be typical to the way a toddler relates to her mother but is inappropriate for college classmates. Although this dynamic is desirable in a therapist-client relationship, it makes for convoluted and confusing friendships.

Living in Self-Deception

We have asked why the "stuff" of the heart comes up, and we should also ask what can keep it repressed. One reason is the human heart's undeniable propensity to avoid suffering. And then when we do suffer we can easily resist receiving insight into our soul. Trials do not automatically result in growth.

Apart from the grace of God we lack the courage to revisit painful memories; we do not have the humility required to confess our sins and immaturity; we are loath to give up our bitterness against those who have hurt us. Consequently, when the mechanism of repression breaks down and stuff starts coming up, we tend to find new ways to push it back down.

The movement in the soul called transference initially affords us a way to put off dealing with whatever has come up. But when it becomes apparent that the transference dynamic is at work, we have the choice either to acknowledge it and begin working through it or to ignore it.

Choosing to deal with it ultimately results in greater maturity; not working through it, however, leads either to a rebuilding of the coping mechanisms that formerly kept the unresolved issues repressed, or to spinning off into an illusory world in which the negative illusions of the transference are substituted for reality. In the latter case our progress toward Christian maturity grinds to a screeching halt.

Sigmund Freud recognized this refusal in some of his patients and called it a "transference-resistance." In these cases he described the transference as being exclusively negative, lacking any positive elements.

Freud contrasted these cases to those having ambivalent components. An example of this hopeful kind of ambivalence is the woman who believes that her therapist is rejecting her as her father once rejected her, while at the same time secretly feeling she is in love with him and clinging to the conviction that he can help her.

Without the positive side of the ambivalence to accompany the negative, Freud felt the possibility for cure was lost: "Where the capacity for transference has become essentially limited to a negative one, as in the case with paranoics, there ceases to be any possibility of influence or cure."[2]

Transference-resistance occurs in nonclinical settings as well. For example, a clergyman related to me his experience of being scrutinized and judged by a woman who served as the bookkeeper of his small country church. She came from a background of being mistreated and betrayed by men and, unknown to the pastor, had a track record of leaving churches in harsh criticism of the pastor.

Over a period of several months she became suspicious of him and accused him of mismanaging the church finances. When the church board looked into the matter they found the pastor to be beyond reproach, despite her unbending insistence of wrongdoing. Meanwhile the pastor was patient with her and, not recognizing the dynamic of transference, continued to use her as bookkeeper. He hoped she could learn to trust him if he gave her enough time and reassurance.

But within a few weeks the situation worsened; her accusations grew more broad and preposterous. Finally, she left the church with threats of suing him. Only after this did the pastor talk to the leaders of her former churches, all of whom reported similar difficulties. Sadly, the vehemence and seriousness of her accusations seemed only to grow as she moved from church to church.

This unfortunate woman was stuck in a pattern of self-deception. In fact, she seemed to thrive on the chaos she caused everywhere she went. She lived in a series of transference-resistance relationships much like the patients for whom Freud held no hope for change.

Our Desperately Sick Hearts

How do we make sense of such behavior? Thankfully, it does not require a degree in psychology. Put simply, we fallen creatures have a great propensity toward finding new ways to avoid what was once repressed. Often we fear the suffering that awaits us if we face reality, including past deprivations, painful memories, and overwhelming emotions.

This impulse to avoid pain by preserving a measure of unreality is an expression of the heart's fallen nature. Speaking of it the prophet Jeremiah once wrote, "The heart is more deceitful than all else and is desperately sick; Who can understand it?" (Jeremiah 17:9, NASB). It is in this context that we should understand transference: It is an expression of the heart's deceitfulness. It is a mistaken, illusory way of interpreting *present* relationships as a defense against facing painful *past* relationships.

I have observed this dynamic in the lives of mature Christians who were beginning to face the most painful parts of their past. Just as the key memories began to surface, they suddenly began to transfer onto those who were best able to help them. In these cases they failed to acknowledge their transferences and thereby to unravel their confused perceptions. Furthermore, they found reasons to break their fellowship with those who could help them, thus remaining frozen in a state of confusion and unreality until such a time as they can successfully work through the repressed difficulty.

I also experienced this battle against self-deception in my transference onto Cindy. When she first confronted me with the fact that there was something terribly wrong with the way that I viewed her, I argued, pleaded, and tried to manipulate her and everyone else into seeing things my way. I stubbornly hung on to my mistaken belief that her actions were the source of my sadness, anxiety, loneliness, and depression.

When finally I admitted that I was misperceiving her, I faced the reality that my present emotional suffering was rooted in my childhood. But I went back and forth between knowing what was true and neurotically ruminating over something that was entirely untrue—how Cindy was to blame for my pain.

My renewed heart, and its desire to love what was true,[3] was in conflict with the deceitful desire of my fallen nature to hold on to what was false. While in prayer I would face some of the infantile pain and receive God's healing touch, and my thinking would clear. But then, perhaps a day later, more pain would surface and I would again relapse into old thought patterns of blaming Cindy. My deceitful heart would again busy itself with litigiously and systematically reviewing her every flaw, real or imagined. In this way I successfully avoided acknowledging my own emotions and facing the memories from which they originated. This battle between the old and new self lasted about five months.

Harboring Pride

The heart's deceitful nature is concerned with more than just simply avoiding painful truths about the self and others. Its sinful impulse also seeks to reshape reality in ways that will serve its prideful, inflated image. Such unconfessed pride in the soul results in a person's inability to let go of misperceptions and mistaken judgments.

A prideful heart resists taking responsibility for sinful attitudes and actions and stands in the way of an objective inventory of the past's painful realities that would shed light on the present confusion. Unfortunately, it also blocks one from accepting help or counsel from other people unless it lines up with the favored image of the self, whether perfect, victimized, or whatever. Tragically, pride even blocks a person's capacity to receive from God, either directly or through the ministry of another.

I have had the sad experience of knowing some who harbor this pride in their hearts. When confronted with the fact of their transference onto another they steadfastly insist that their childhood was happy, even though they once keenly knew of their parents' failures and the pain of early circumstances.

In one remarkable case I was acquainted with a middle-aged man who over the course of a year repeatedly told me of his mistreatment by his parents, sisters, and grandparents. He was routinely left out of family events, mistrusted without reason, and disciplined unfairly, all for the stated reason that he was a boy.

A few years into our acquaintance, and just after the death of his father, I met with him to pray about a difficulty that had arisen between him and his pastor. As I asked questions about his family of origin and tried to relate them to his present misperceptions of the pastor, he suddenly changed the story of his childhood. Now he insisted that he had always felt loved by his parents and was especially grateful to his father for all that he had learned from him.

Furthermore, he took great offense when I reminded him of the unhappy facts that he had previously shared with me. He now excused his family's treatment of him as related to their "blue-collar" mindset and their ethnic origins. Likewise he excused his behavior at his workplace, which had resulted in his losing his job. Instead he blamed his employer's "prejudice" against the way he chose to express his anger. And now he was bitterly angry with his pastor for the steps taken against him for reasons of protection.

In all of this, the man had only fleeting moments of remorse for his behavior. He was unable to confess his pride, much less his anger, and therefore could not take even the first step in resolving his transference onto his pastor.

Resistant to Love

Pride also stands in the way of the heart's opening up to receive healing because the needed receptive posture is antithetical to pride. For example, a man in transference who suffered a deprivation of his mother's love may refuse to receive the prayer and loving touch that he desperately needs from other people. Instead, he clings to the idea that God will heal him in the privacy of his own prayer times, so that he never has to place himself in a vulnerable and humble position toward others.

Writing of this human propensity to resist love, moral philosopher Josef Pieper says,

> Within man there is a tendency to fend off the creative love that unasked and undeservedly has given him his own existence. At bottom all love is undeserved. We can neither earn it nor promote it; it is always a pure gift. . . . But there seems to be in man something like an aversion for receiving gifts. No one is wholly unfamiliar with the thought: I don't want anything for nothing! And this emotion comes uncannily close to the other: I don't want to be "loved," and certainly not for no reason! It was Nietzsche who made the acute remark that "people addicted to honor," that is people for whom their own importance is chiefly what matters, are "resistant to being loved." And C. S. Lewis says that absolutely undeserved love is certainly what we need but not at all the kind

of love we want. "We want to be loved for our cleverness, beauty, generosity, fairness, usefulness."[4]

Pride, then, not only fights against acknowledging transference but holds us back from receiving the grace God longs to extend. Only when pride is confessed and overcome can the Holy Spirit use the transference to reeducate our cognitive faculties to enable us to perceive things as they really are. Likewise the love that God desires to send—a divine tonic for human deprivation—can be received only in a posture of humility.

The Lord instructs the prideful, complaining Israelites,

> I am the LORD your God,
>   who brought you up out of Egypt.
>   *Open wide your mouth and I will fill it.*
>
> But my people would not listen to me;
>   Israel would not submit to me.
> So I gave them over to their stubborn hearts
>   to follow their own devices.
>
> If my people would but listen to me,
>   if Israel would follow my ways,
> how quickly would I subdue their enemies
>   and turn my hand against their foes!
> Those who hate the LORD would cringe before him,
>   and their punishment would last forever.
> But *you would be fed with the finest of wheat;*
>   *with honey from the rock I would satisfy you.*
>
>   Psalm 81:10–16, emphasis mine

As he did for the Israelites, so too does the Lord hold out to his suffering children his full provision for our deepest needs. But we must acknowledge our need and humbly receive, with grateful hearts, the nurture, comfort, and sustenance God sends to us.

To receive the healing that God freely extends, we must learn to accept it in the form that he chooses, rather than demanding that he fulfill our needs in ways that we envision. More often than not, the healing that lasts is not that which comes upon us suddenly and dramatically like a thunderbolt from heaven. Those who expect—and even demand—such things from God must often consciously lay down their notions about how their healing will come.

In part 3 we will look further at the ways of dealing with and overcoming transference through common, everyday spiritual disciplines such as forgiveness and repentance. But first we turn in part 2 to the hallmarks of transference in the church.

PART 2

Transference in the Church

6

Overt and Litigious Encounters

lthough the term *transference* was not coined until the beginning of the twentieth century, the behavior that it describes has been going on for centuries. In fact, the whole of Scripture narrates the history of our need as fallen human beings to distance ourselves from what hurts us, whether it is the painful acknowledgment of our sin against another or the dread of facing the way someone has injured us. Story after story in the Scriptures demonstrates the great lengths we will go to avoid and escape suffering. This is the stuff of transference.

Passages in the Bible also reveal the destruction wreaked by transference onto Christian leaders. As we turn in part 2 to considering the effect of this harmful phenomenon in churches, we begin with a look at its influence on a well-known leader from centuries ago.

Mighty Men Turned Motley

Returning home from battle, King David and his men suffered a terrible shock. Upon entering their village they saw that it had been destroyed by fire and learned that the Amalekites had taken their wives and children captive. Understandably, David and his men were overcome with grief and anger; they "wept aloud until they had no strength left to weep."[1]

Quite unexpectedly, however, the men redirected their hatred away from the Amalekites onto King David, the very one who had been weeping with them and who had also suffered loss. All the anger they had felt toward the Amalekites fell on David, and their emotions swelled into murderous rage against him. So great was their fury, in fact, that David feared for his life: "David was greatly distressed because the men were talking of stoning him."

This sudden shifting of blame on the part of King David's faithful followers lacks logic. But this turnabout illustrates the way people who are in pain commonly direct their anger toward those nearest to them, rather than to the responsible party. The men found it easier to blame David than to seek God for the strength to rise from their grief and face their real enemy, the Amalekites.

This is the very essence of transference. When sorrow from the past has not been resolved through forgiving and receiving forgiveness, the soul seeks out another "sin bearer." In this story, the men sought to assuage their fury by making David bear the sin of the Amalekites. Had he not stopped them, they would have brought about justice in their own way by killing him.

Job Hazards for Leaders

David's story illustrates the way leaders are especially prone to becoming the objects of transference. The violence of David's men toward him is shocking because we see elsewhere their unique devotion to him. The genuine love between them was, in fact, a precursor to the transference because David's relationship with his men resembled the trusting relationship of a parent and child. Their mutual suffering during Saul's persecution of David had produced a special bond.

Also, like a parent, David was an authority figure. This combination of mutual trust and authority, so foundational to effective leadership, provided a perfect environment for transference to flourish.

Any relationship that resembles the affinity between parent and child is vulnerable. For example, my friendship with Cindy was well suited for transference in two ways: the trust growing between us as a result of our praying and ministering together; and my unhealthy emotional dependence on her, which mimicked a child's dependence on a mother. This reconstruction of the parent-child relationship can also occur in marriages, in work groups and office relationships, between doctors and patients, in church staffs, and on ministry teams.

After a few experiences like David's, some Christian leaders react by isolating themselves or staying aloof. They attempt to keep painful projections at bay by avoiding warm, trusting relationships with those whom they lead.

But transference can occur even in the absence of genuine relating. For example, the leaders of Pastoral Care Ministry schools can become the objects of strong, almost instantaneous projections and transferences from complete strangers because they symbolize fatherhood, motherhood, and authority. These symbols alone are sufficient to bring forth a wounded person's unresolved difficulties.

Another reason why Christian leaders are particularly prone to become the objects of this relational dynamic is their call to minister to and alongside the brokenhearted. For instance, David's men who followed him through the years of persecution and who at the end of David's life received the epitaph "David's mighty men" were a motley bunch. Scripture describes them in their early days together: "All those who were in distress or debt or discontented gathered around him, and he became their leader" (1 Samuel 22:2).

Surely David knew from the beginning the risk he was taking with these men. Nonetheless, he welcomed and trusted them as sons and brothers. Likewise, people with problems of every possible kind thronged around Jesus. Like David, he did not hesitate to invite these needy ones to be his disciples.

And the same is true today. The Lord seems to delight in using the poor in spirit to accomplish the work of his kingdom. Therefore, the possibility and even probability of transference by those who are hurting and immature is one of the risks leaders must be prepared to take. Until and while these needy ones receive healing, those who minister to and with them risk becoming the objects of transference. Thus the challenge for leaders is not only to learn how to identify this dynamic, but to insure that the work of the kingdom of God is done in spite of it, and even through it.

Church Conflicts

Another factor leaders need to reckon with is the condition of the church in the age in which we live. No longer do people hold an unqualified respect for clergy as before; this esteem once held in check vindictive inclinations. Public scandals involving prominent Christian leaders have also contributed to the widespread disrespect, as has the democratic value of free speech run amok when it becomes a license for hypercriticism, gossip, and calumny.

This new social reality was brought home to me in conversations with Roman Catholics in Europe where men and women in religious orders yet wear garb in the fashion of the Middle Ages. There the clergy are still held in high regard, especially among the devout. They explained to me that in their churches, the priests almost never become the objects of transference, but rather the focus is on the lay leaders. And although there were plenty of problems with transference, the clergy still know a measure of protection because of the high esteem of their office.

By contrast, Christian leaders in the United States cannot count on any immunity to transference due to their status. In fact, the opposite is true; they are more likely to experience it.

This is further evidenced by the prevalence and acceptance of conflict in many churches. Irreconcilable disputes between pastors and their congregations seem to be epidemic, especially in Protestant churches. *Leadership,* a well-respected journal for pastors and leaders, devoted an entire issue to describing the problem. The statistics they present are startling: "According to the survey, 62 percent of forced-out pastors said the church that forced them out had done it before. Of those who said their church had pushed out their predecessors, 41 percent indicated the church had done it more than twice."[2]

The bewildered tone in this issue probably results from a failure to understand and identify transference in church conflicts. The cure for such an epidemic may not be simple, but begins with understanding what transference typically looks like in a church setting.

I have noticed two distinct patterns of transference. The first is *overt,* characterized by *litigiousness* and frequently mistaken for ordinary conflict. More difficult to discern is the *covert* type of transference, characterized by *factiousness.* Transferences of this kind, described in the next chapter, may work their destruction over a number of years and yet remain completely undetected.

The Endless Arguments of Litigiousness

After hearing me speak about transference, a pastor told me about the situation that had arisen in his small country parish. He was about to lose his job—or in exasperation give up the ministry on his own accord—over what started as a petty complaint against him.

The troubles began with a criticism by the church secretary that he did not keep proper order in the church's supply closet. The secretary busied herself with searching out every scrap of evidence to prove that the pastor was a failure as an administrator and then presented her findings to anyone who would listen. Eventually entire church council meetings were devoted to examining this evidence.

Then after several months, the discussion shifted its focus and became a debate over the Scripture's teaching regarding pastors. The debates were primarily over whether or not the Bible prescribes that pastors should have administrative skills, or whether it teaches that administration is a different office altogether. This, of course, led to heated discussions about the church budget, whether the church could afford two pastors, and who was to blame for the lack of funds.

Eventually the entire church was preoccupied and polarized over this issue. For more than a year the pastor spent most of his time defending himself from attacks on his character and qualifications for ministry. He felt nit-picked to a maddening degree as his every word and smallest action, not to mention his real mistakes and shortcomings, were psychoanalyzed, "judged" by the Scriptures, and discussed.

This pastor's story is an example of the litigiousness commonly associated with transference. In it the pastor's secretary was preoccupied with building her case against him, much as if she were a lawyer or detective. Her litigious preoccupation with the pastor was actually a form of neurotic mental obsession. Not only that, but she spread her hypercritical attitude throughout the congregation as she endlessly conversed and argued about the pastor's shortcomings.

Finally the pastor himself was drawn into the litigiousness as he, point by point, attempted to defend himself to her and to the church council. These intense dialogues and debates were strangely satisfying to the secretary, who had a great need for connection with other people. Her need, in fact, arose from her parents' divorce when she was a teenager and the subsequent years of listening to her mother complain about her father. Not only was she driven by her anger toward her father, but she acted out the behavior her mother had modeled to her.

Thriving on Conflict

Sam's transference is another example of the way this dynamic can lead to confrontations that strangely satisfy a person's need for connection with other people. When Sam was part of a church leadership team he requested an appointment with his pastor to discuss certain grievances. As the two were longtime friends the pastor happily granted his request, confident that they could work things out.

During their first meeting the pastor listened to Sam's accusations for four hours, after which he tried to clear up any misunderstanding or miscommunication. Sam was emotional throughout, first raving with anger and then crying in contrition. The session concluded with an exchange of forgiveness and a renewed pledge to work together in the ministry.

Not recognizing that his friend was in transference, the pastor believed the difficulty had been resolved. But a week later he received another troubling call from Sam. A second long meeting was held in which they covered the identical grievances that had been discussed in the first meeting.

Finally, after three or four such meetings, the pastor realized that the situation was only getting worse. He kindly but firmly turned down Sam's requests for further appointments and made arrangements for others to meet with him. Sam was deeply offended and eventually left the church.

In retrospect, the pastor realized that Sam had been in transference onto him. And he saw that the meetings that Sam insisted upon were an attempt to connect with him on an exaggerated emotional plane in lieu of a healthy relationship. Sam, he understood too late, was thriving on conflict.

Misusing the Scriptures

Using the Scriptures as a weapon to accuse and judge another person is a hallmark of transference among Christians. My litigious case against Cindy clearly illustrates this: I scrutinized her in the light of Scripture much as a lawyer researches laws and past rulings in preparation for a court battle. I also gathered witnesses, so to speak, as I talked about Cindy with mutual friends. And when at last I confronted her, I used the Scriptures to back up my claims.

Likewise, in the pastors' cases above, the people in transference against them used the Bible as a law by which to judge. Those who are litigious often believe they have special insight into both the Scriptures and the character of those they are scrutinizing.

Another way the Scriptures are commonly misused is a faulty application of the model presented in Matthew 18:15–17 (NRSV) for confronting sin:

> If another member of the church sins against you, go and point out the fault when the two of you are alone. If the member listens to you, you have regained that one. But if you are not listened to, take one or two others along with you, so that every word may be confirmed by the evidence of two or three witnesses. If the member refuses to listen to them, tell it to the church; and if the offender

refuses to listen even to the church, let such a one be to you as a Gentile and a tax collector.

In these cases the object of the transference is confronted with a long list of grievances, most of which are exaggerated or altogether fictitious. The Christian leader finds himself in an impossible situation. If he tries to be open and humble, he learns that any admission he makes will most certainly be used against him later. But if he refuses to admit to the accusations, the one transferring feels justified in bringing other people into the conflict as witnesses.

The application of Jesus' teaching is inappropriate here. The real sin that needs to be confessed, and the real conflict that needs to be resolved, is not with the pastor but with someone from the accuser's past history.

After the transference has been acknowledged, Matthew 18 can be applied appropriately as the tables are turned and the sins against the pastor are confronted. Then the sins of gossip, slander, litigiousness, factiousness, envy, and so forth can be dealt with using this model.

Mediation Wrongly Applied

Another common mistake when attempting to resolve a situation of transference is employing a conflict resolution method that focuses on communication, often facilitated by a mediator. For this model to succeed both parties must be objective and rational. But because transference is by nature subjective and irrational, the model will not work.

In fact, the very act of calling in a mediator serves to validate the accuser's agenda. Furthermore it gives the false impression that a conflict exists in which both parties are to share the blame. It also may suggest that the mediator is conducting a legitimate investigation into someone's character.

Thus, to involve a mediator before the transference is named can actually make things worse, particularly for the one receiving the transference. In truth a mediator cannot help until the transference, and all the sins that issue from it, are acknowledged and confessed. Only then will he or she be able to facilitate real, objective problem-solving conversations.

Commenting on this mistaken way of dealing with transference, Leanne Payne states:

> I have found that the inability to comprehend these matters on the part of the people surrounding the needy one is often the greatest cross to bear in dealing with these matters. When this lack of discernment is shared by Christians in authority, the person's sickness is often irremediably affirmed. Actually, it makes transference (that which can lead to healing for the sufferer) an intolerable burden for those being slandered by it.
>
> Some pastors and church leaders, grievously in turmoil because of such transferences, attempt to deal with them not as the difficulty they in fact are but as problems to be discussed endlessly and dealt with "according to the Scriptures." Time after time, they throw their weight on the side of the erring one, and libel as well the object of that one's transference. Incredibly enough, even some Christian psychologists and counselors do the same.[3]

As she notes, transferences can remain hidden even to those closest to the ones in transference. This is all the more true when the one in transference engages in an undercover mission of destruction.

7

Covert and Factious Liaisons

We have just seen examples of litigious transference that are face-to-face confrontations. Those who are being transferred onto know who is accusing them and why. But in other cases of transference, those being attacked have no opportunity to defend themselves. In these scenarios the accuser works undercover, rarely confronting the target directly. To carry on this covert work requires a generous amount of cunning, the talent to preserve secrecy, and a strong intuitive capacity to detect others' emotional weakness and vulnerability.

These unknown adversaries quickly ascertain whether or not a person can be drawn into the transference without realizing what is happening. They also avoid drawing in any others who might bring down their veil of secrecy. And they are able to secure a great deal of loyalty from the people whom they involve in their transferences. Those who fit this profile are often gifted and successful, having earned a place of respect and trust within their spheres of influence. As such they are the last ones anyone would suspect of harboring ill will or undermining a ministry.

The Scripture has a name for this kind of daunting, dark expression of intelligence: *factiousness,* or, as the word is translated in the New International Version, *divisiveness*. Of all the sins that issue out of transference, this is the most destructive.

Rape, Murder, and Intrigue

From a biblical standpoint, factiousness is the sin of recruiting others into one's grievances against an individual with the intent of usurping leadership or unseating them from their position. The classic example is Absalom's sin against David, found in 2 Samuel.[1]

The story of Absalom's factious intrigues surrounding his father, King David, began after his half-brother, Amnon, raped his sister Tamar. For reasons not told in the biblical account, David was slow to respond to this terrible situation. Absalom, however, was understandably impatient with his father's inaction and wanted to see justice done. Two years after the incident, he took matters into his own hands and had Amnon murdered.

The Scriptures do not say whether Absalom tried to confront his father prior to Amnon's murder; certainly there was no chance afterward as Absalom fled immediately to Geshur. After three years of silence King David summoned his son back to Jerusalem. Absalom returned but avoided his father for two years. Perhaps David was content with this arrangement, as it seems that Joab, the king's general, felt it was his duty to keep Absalom from David.

Eventually, however, the father and son met. The Scriptures recount that "the king summoned Absalom, and he came in and bowed down with his face to the ground before the king. And the king kissed Absalom" (2 Samuel 14:33). It seems that David had forgiven Absalom and was ready to end their estrangement.

But as the story unfolds, it becomes clear that Absalom's anger and resentment toward his father had not abated in the least:

> He would get up early and stand by the side of the road leading to the city gate. Whenever anyone came with a complaint to be placed before the king for a decision, Absalom would call out to him, "What town are you from?" He would answer, "Your servant is from one of the tribes of Israel." Then Absalom would say to him, "Look, your claims are valid and proper, but there is no representative of the

king to hear you." And Absalom would add, "If only I were appointed judge in the land! Then everyone who has a complaint or case could come to me and I would see that he gets justice."

Also, whenever anyone approached him to bow down before him, Absalom would reach out his hand, take hold of him and kiss him. Absalom behaved in this way toward all the Israelites who came to the king asking for justice, and so he stole the hearts of the men of Israel.

2 Samuel 15:2–6

Absalom employed his covert campaign at the city gates for four years. Having secured favor with the crowds, he asked his father to allow him to go to Hebron, "to fulfill a vow I made to the LORD." The king, unaware of Absalom's true plans, sent him in peace. The story continues:

Then Absalom sent secret messengers throughout the tribes of Israel to say, "As soon as you hear the sound of the trumpets, then say, 'Absalom is king in Hebron.'" Two hundred men from Jerusalem had accompanied Absalom. They had been invited as guests and went quite innocently, knowing nothing about the matter. While Absalom was offering sacrifices, he also sent for Ahithophel the Gilonite, David's counselor, to come from Giloh, his hometown. And so the conspiracy gained strength, and Absalom's following kept on increasing.

2 Samuel 15:10–12

After much bloodshed, David prevailed over the conspiracy and preserved his kingship. But the story ended in tragedy for both David and Absalom: Joab and his men killed Absalom as he hung helplessly from a tree limb after a battle. Absalom died without his father's blessing, and David was left to grieve the death of his son: "O my son Absalom! My son, my son Absalom! If only I had died instead of you—O Absalom, my son, my son!" (2 Samuel 18:33).

A Crippling Phenomenon

Although we can be slow to recognize it, the factiousness that divides our churches today and leads many ministers to resign is much akin to the ugly display of anger, treachery, and intrigue in Absalom's story. And although contemporary factiousness almost never turns into bloodshed as it did so frequently in David's time, the violence done to the pastors, their families, and those in their congregations is devastating.

For example, after a battle with such treachery many pastors lose their confidence in and passion for ministry. Others, to their horror, discover that their next church is ruled by the same sort of faction. This is especially true in churches where a small group of lay people gain control by stirring up factiousness and ousting one leader after another.

David Goetz in *Leadership* magazine calls these congregations "repeat-offender" churches and notes that what animates them is "the power of a few."

> Forty-three percent of forced-out pastors said a "faction" pushed them out, and 71 percent of those indicated that the "faction" forcing them out numbered ten or less. These tiny wolf packs often hoard the inside information. Only 20 percent of pastors who were forced out said the real reason for their leaving was made known to the congregation.[2]

Such pastors who are forced from their churches can easily lose their bearings; they are unable to sort out what happened and are left doubting themselves, their abilities, and their call to ministry. Those who find new positions often feel crippled in their capacity to teach, lead, and shepherd others. Some leave public ministry altogether.

Bystanders also suffer damaging effects, especially in churches where they watch one pastor after another crumble under criticism and then leave. These onlookers are often unaware of the exact nature of the dissatisfaction with the pastor and are rarely given the opportunity to hear both sides of the story. They only have hypercritical information circulated by the factious group.

Many of these observers feel abandoned and confused, not knowing whom to trust; over time they may become disillusioned with leaders in general. Some, of course, catch on to what is happening and look for a different church. Like their ousted leaders, however, many of them find that the next church has the same problem.

This phenomenon has reached epidemic proportions in American churches. Today it seems accepted that certain small groups will always seek to turn their churches into little kingdoms where they rule uncontested and where the true church leaders either learn to submit or they resign.

What remains less understood, however, is the role that transference plays in these situations. To understand this often unseen dynamic is to perceive church struggles as being more than simply contests for power and control. The complexity of human motivation is greater than a mere drive toward domination.

Piggybacking

Transference is not the explanation for every church split nor the real reason behind every pastor's resignation, but in many instances it lies at the crux of church problems. The reason for its central role relates to the propensity for a person in transference to ignite transferences in others, whether knowingly or unconsciously. And as two or more people band together with a common transference onto the same person, the power to wreak havoc increases.

Leanne Payne calls this the piggybacking phenomenon:

> Another grievous thing I have observed is the "piggybacking" phenomenon common in unacknowledged transferences within the church. People caught in resistance can never stop slandering (sometimes only very subtly) and they intuitively know how to constellate latent-transferences in other needy souls (as well as a critical spirit in otherwise healthy people) toward the object of their transference.[3]

Those likely to spark transferences in other people generally harbor hostile, often paranoid feelings about the objects of their transferences. Strangely, however, they are usually only vaguely aware of these negative feelings; their anger only shows up as the proverbial tip of the iceberg. But underneath is an overwhelming, red-hot rage against a parent that has been unconsciously misplaced onto the object of their transference.

With their negative emotions repressed, they can successfully draw others into their transferences. For if they displayed their negative feelings openly, people would be repelled, not attracted. Thus they can gather unto themselves those who will vicariously give vent to these repressed emotions.

They commonly target five types of people to involve in their transferences: (1) those whose emotional and intellectual boundaries are weak and who will take on the thoughts and emotions of another as if their own; (2) immature Christians who lack discernment but respect their authority or position; (3) those closest in relationship to the object of the transference; (4) those who overidentify and overempathize with sin in wounded people, and (5) those whose emotional difficulties are similar to their own.

The methods they use to rally people to their cause are varied. But three key patterns tend to recur in one situation after another. The first is bringing discontented people together around an issue that seems positive and spiritual. The second is persuading others to embark on a moral campaign to expose and confront a leader's flaws, whether real or imagined. And the third is taking up a counselor's persona in order to "counsel" several people who are all in transference onto the same person. Let us look at these in more detail.

Scenario 1: Factiousness Disguised as a Good Cause

Factiousness can be cleverly disguised when a person draws a group together around an issue that seems positive and spiritual. The focus is generally along the lines of the leader's real interests. For example, a person might assemble people to talk about ministry to the poor, based on her authentic concerns. The energy behind her efforts, however, will be the emotions of the unacknowledged transference, not the prompting of the Holy Spirit.

She will gather together some who are genuinely interested in the poor. But others, especially those also in transference, will participate simply because they are attracted by the atmosphere of discontent. And rather than moving forward to serve the needy, the group will focus on motivating the pastor and the rest of the church to care more about the poor.

Usually they fail to get any project up and running. Instead they succeed in galvanizing critical, judgmental attitudes toward the pastor, other leaders, or the church at large. Meanwhile, the person who drew the group together will be held in high esteem as one "having a heart for the poor." In contrast, the pastor's interest in the poor will be viewed as inadequate or feigned.

Unlike one who simply needs to let go of an idealized image of a pastor, the person in transference has a strong need to expose the pastor's inadequacies, whether real or imagined, to as many people as possible. Behind this lies her anger at an inadequate parent and her need to forgive.

Scenario 2: Factiousness Disguised as a Moral Crusade

A second expression of factiousness occurs when a person in transference persuades others to carry on a moral crusade against a leader. He impresses upon them their "moral responsibility" to expose and confront a leader's flaws—whether or not of real consequence. Singling out well-respected members of the congregation, he educates them through gossip and slander about the leader's "problems." Eventually he may ask them to use their influence to call attention to the matter.

For example, a man in transference launched a campaign against the senior pastor of a large church whom he believed had a problem with inordinate anger. The man in transference had known terrible physical and emotional abuse throughout his childhood; the amount of rage he projected onto the pastor was therefore of unusual magnitude.

Some whom he recruited were also in transference and jumped at the opportunity to air their grievances. But he also enlisted some who were well-meaning but naive, much like the two hundred men who went with Absalom to Hebron.[4] These people hoped that their efforts would help the pastor to acknowledge his problem and secure the help he needed.

Little did they know that the one leading the campaign was in transference and therefore would be satisfied with nothing less than the leader's disgrace and removal from ministry. Restoration was not an option. His diabolical motives, however, were well hidden from those he recruited. And later, as the pastor was forced out of the church, they were shocked at the ruthless, merciless outcome of the situation.

Strangely, the person at the core of this type of group transference often goes unnoticed by the congregation at large. As the case is built against the leader, the main one in transference stays hidden because he or she enlists others to function more publicly.

Scenario 3: Factiousness Disguised as a Therapeutic Relationship

Friendships that appear to be counselor-counselee relationships can also serve as hidden vehicles through which factiousness spreads. These can even be professional therapeutic relationships but are more often found informally among lay people. Here the one in transference takes on the role of a "counselor" toward those who have real or imagined grievances with a leader.

Often she will target a vulnerable person, initiating a conversation by asking leading questions that open the way for gossip and slander. With a few apparently benign queries, she can determine whether she has found someone who resonates with her grievances, all the while hiding her own heart.

For example, she might ask, "Does it ever bother you that Rev. Jones never makes pastoral visits?" or "Have you ever had any trouble getting along with our minister?" She will wait to hear something that expresses her own feelings toward the pastor. Then, rather than empathizing in a way that would reveal her own hostility, she will say with concern, "I can see you are really in pain; Rev. Jones must have done something to hurt you," or "Others have reported this same thing to me."

She therefore feeds her counselee's discontent by reporting details from others' experiences that will further validate his or her angry feelings. In effect she helps her counselee take on her own grievances and those of others. Soon the person will be heavily burdened by carrying the compounded resentments of several people.

These situations have the appearance of being objective because of the counselor's ability to hide her emotions. In fact, they are completely subjective because the counselor asks questions and introduces information entirely motivated by her own emotions. The counselee is manipulated into expressing the counselor's hidden feelings.

Because emotional boundaries become fuzzy and unclear in these situations, a false sense of unity and intimacy often results. For example, the friendship may involve long conversations about the object of the transference, much as good friends can spend hours talking about a mutual interest.

But because the commonality of the friendship between the counselor and counselee is based on something that is delusional, the result is a sick pseudofriendship. Those who have difficulty making and sustaining healthy relationships are especially vulnerable to this way of unhealthy relating. Such friendships deteriorate quickly once the transference is exposed.

Each of these three scenarios displays an element of vicarious transference. In essence, the one in transference manipulates others to act out the transference on his or her behalf—all to destructive effects. We turn next to an example of vicarious transference hidden under the banner of friendship.

8

Vicarious Transference

Vicarious transference, as we have seen, may go unnoticed and unsuspected for long periods of time, even years. As Leanne Payne says, "These vicarious transferences are the most difficult of all to discern because we can see no visible signs. These persons manifest no hostile or paranoid feelings toward the object. Only their positive, loving face is ever seen."

Commenting on the wounding effects of this dynamic, she writes,

> Christians who are split off from both their feelings and infantile rage genuinely love the object of their transference. . . . These people tend to stay close to the object of their transference while simultaneously drawing out latent transferences in others. It can take years to find out what is really going on. This is piggybacking with a vengeance. And in connection with ground-breaking ministries, this may well constitute spiritual warfare at its height.[1]

An example of one who loved her object of transference even while bringing forth transferences in other people can be seen in the case of Shannon and Jane.

A Hidden Cloud

Jane was a well-known and respected Bible teacher and pastoral counselor in a large church. With children grown and out of the home, she was able to devote her full energy to her ministry. Like many women who become the objects of strong transferences, she beautifully embodied the nurturing qualities of femininity and motherhood.

Shannon, the mother of three small children, was moderately depressed and just beginning to grow as a Christian when she met Jane. She shared with her new acquaintance how she had suffered terrible neglect throughout her childhood at the hands of her mentally ill mother. With Jane's help she grew quickly, shaking off her depression, and came to be highly respected as a capable person. For those few who knew her history she seemed self-confident and undaunted by a painful upbringing.

Shannon soon became an active lay leader in the church, helping Jane in many capacities. Over the years the two of them grew to be friends, with Jane becoming a grandmother figure to Shannon's family.

Yet throughout the early years of their friendship, and side by side with her love and appreciation for Jane, Shannon wrestled with vague, inexplicable feelings of mistrust and anger toward her. She also envied the spiritual effectiveness of Jane's ministry. On the whole she repressed these feelings, hiding them from those around her.

Throughout these years of Shannon and Jane's friendship, Jane suffered as the object of a number of devastating transferences. Involved with them, sadly, were several people whom Jane had deeply trusted. But despite her determination to remedy these situations, many took a puzzling turn for the worse. It began to appear that Jane was an uncommonly easy target for transferences, which she rarely saw favorably resolved.

But what Jane did not know was the extent of Shannon's involvement in these situations. Shannon was secretly undermining Jane's efforts to deal effectively with these problems—in fact, she was escalating the transferences. This only came to light some years later when Shannon moved to another state to be nearer to her husband's aging parents.

Sowing Discontent

After the move Shannon sorely missed Jane, the ministry they once shared, and the whole church community. By this time all of her children were school age or out of the home and she had little to keep herself busy. She began to be depressed and realized that the old depression could once again overtake her.

All the while she missed Jane, but the underlying anger she had kept hidden became more and more difficult to ignore. She also became increasingly jealous of those who were now more closely related to Jane. Nonetheless Shannon kept up with her old friend and often traveled back to see her.

Over time, however, her critical thoughts and negative feelings toward Jane increased dramatically. But despite her familiarity with the dynamic of transference, Shannon could not or would not acknowledge that this dynamic might be present in her relations to Jane. So great was her resistance to admitting her own transference, in fact, that she was reluctant even to accept transference as a valid psychological concept.

Her ambivalence came to light one day when Shannon teleponed Jane's secretary, Margaret, at the church office. Margaret had been working closely with Jane for a year when she received this call. Although she had spoken with Shannon occasionally before, this phone call was altogether different from the previous calls—it was apparent from the beginning that Shannon had a strong agenda.

It began on an uncomfortably personal note when Shannon, her voice full of sympathy, told Margaret that she had been thinking about her a great deal. She seemed to be gravely concerned with Margaret's welfare and asked probing questions that presupposed Margaret would encounter serious difficulties in relating to Jane. When Margaret could not provide any information to substantiate these concerns, Shannon went on to ask her about Jane's other relationships. She plainly insinuated that others were having serious difficulties with Jane.

Margaret was taken off guard by Shannon's sudden and intense interest in her life. In response to the probing questions, she candidly admitted that in getting to know Jane she had struggled with some projection and transference onto her. But Margaret added that she had worked through this successfully and now enjoyed not only a good working relationship but a growing friendship with Jane.

Once Margaret disclosed her struggles with transference onto Jane, Shannon became notably agitated, even angry. She strongly intimated that Jane was transferring onto her, Margaret. Such a possibility had never crossed Margaret's mind and she did not know how to respond. She finally replied by assuring Shannon that Jane had been very transparent and seemed quite willing to confess her sins and shortcomings as she was made aware of them.

Their conversation ended as Shannon reiterated that she knew well the kind of "special support" that Margaret would need in order to work with Jane. She offered to counsel her anytime about these matters.

Onset then Retreat of the Darkness

Margaret felt extremely anxious and fearful after this phone call. For several hours she was bombarded with feelings of meaninglessness and irrational thoughts: What if Shannon is right? What if I can't trust my perceptions of Jane? Can I trust my perceptions of others whom I trust? Along with these anxious, fearful thoughts came a suffocating sense of spiritual oppression that Margaret found hard to shake.

In the midst of these emotions Margaret was able to discern that transference was involved; she therefore knew that the source of the irrational thoughts was not from within her. Realizing that Shannon had purposefully interjected these fears into her thinking, she understood that she was suffering from the fierce spiritual oppression that had accompanied them.

Margaret prayed and asked the Lord to wash her mind of any dark spiritual influence and to forgive her for entertaining the lying, slanderous thoughts even for a moment. She also acknowledged the way that Shannon had hooked into her anxiety about relating to women and asked for special grace and wisdom to overcome the spiritual battle. After these prayers, most of the overwhelming flood of darkness retreated.

Once her fearful feelings abated, Margaret was angry with Shannon for placing her in the path of spiritual danger. The phone call seemed a deliberate attempt to inject doubt and suspicion into her thinking about Jane. In pondering the possible consequences of taking in Shannon's paranoid thoughts and making them her own, she realized that she could have been sucked into Shannon's transference onto Jane. In due time this would have eroded her trust in Jane, which in turn would have negatively affected their ability to minister together.

Margaret was also angry on Jane's behalf, as Shannon's call seemed a callous act of treachery and a betrayal of longstanding trust. Even the timing seemed diabolical, for it came shortly before Jane was scheduled to minister at an important meeting out of town. Margaret began to wonder about the implications: How many others had been taken in by Shannon's transference? How long had this been going on? To what extent had the slander been circulated? Just thinking about it was suffocating.

A remarkable spiritual tension seemed apparent to Margaret. She became aware of the pressure to hide all of this from Jane, perhaps to try to deal with it by herself. In this it seemed that Margaret was being tempted to a wrong kind of secrecy and to the sin of pride.

As Margaret prayed, she sensed that it was important to tell Jane about the incident right away, despite the distraction it might bring to Jane's preparations for her upcoming speaking engagement. Margaret believed that the lingering sense of spiritual oppression would dissipate as she brought the matter out into the open. And, as she anticipated, it did. When they talked, Jane told Margaret about a similar call from a few years back that another one of her close associates had received from Shannon.

Soon thereafter, it became clear that Shannon was the common connection point for a number of people who were transferring onto Jane. Some of them were receiving professional psychological care or were therapists themselves, yet all turned to Shannon as the one to talk to about their "problems" with Jane.

Unfortunately, none of them discerned what was really happening, and they accepted into themselves Shannon's fear and anger toward Jane. As this mixed together with their own latent issues, many of them transferred demonstratively onto Jane. In this way Shannon expressed her transference vicariously.

School of Virtue; School of Vice

Shannon was able to secure great personal loyalty from those she drew into her circle as she extended herself to them as friend and counselor. Her circle of counselees became a secret society of sorts with two commonly held tenets—their loyalty to Shannon and their preoccupation with scrutinizing Jane. Together they engaged in amateurish psychoanalysis not only of Jane but of her friends and associates as well.

Ironically, Jane had extended warm, true friendship to nearly every person in this group over the years, most notably to Shannon. But each of them harbored deep and sometimes paranoid mistrust of others, which held them back from fully reciprocating Jane's friendship. Strangely, however, they were able to enter for a time into a convoluted friendship with Shannon. As long as they remained in the sphere of her influence they were confirmed in their illusory ways of viewing Jane. They were thus held back from dealing with their own painful issues.

In *The Four Loves* C. S. Lewis writes of the power of friendship to strengthen persons in the way of truth *or* illusion:

> Even now, at whatever age, we all know the perilous charm of a shared hatred or grievance. . . . Alone among unsympathetic companions, I hold certain views and standards timidly, half ashamed to avow them and half doubtful if they can after all be right. Put me back among my Friends and in half an hour—in ten minutes— these same views and standards become once more indisputable. The opinion of this little circle, while I am in it, outweighs that of a thousand outsiders: as Friendship strengthens, it will do this even when my Friends are far away.

... Theirs is the praise we really covet and the blame we really dread. The little pockets of early Christians survived because they cared exclusively for the love of "the brethren" and stopped their ears to the opinion of the Pagan society all round them. But a circle of criminals, cranks, or perverts survives in just the same way; by becoming deaf to the opinion of the outer world, by discounting it as the chatter of outsiders who "don't understand."

... Friendship (as the ancients saw) can be a school of virtue; but also (as they did not see) a school of vice.[2]

In the case of Shannon's vicarious transference, the power of friendship to confirm hurting people in wrong ways of perceiving the world is tragically evident. Her friends encouraged one another in mutual delusion; they became a "school of vice," to use Lewis's apt description.

Because this dynamic was so powerful, it was nearly impossible for those associated with Shannon to work through their transferences, even when they earnestly desired to do so. Their convoluted fellowship, rather than calling them into greater Christ-likeness, blocked the pathway to maturity and even caused them to regress into greater immaturity.

In sharp contrast, of course, is the model of fellowship presented in the Scriptures, wherein we are instructed to base our relationships on truthfulness. The apostle John writes, "If we walk in the light, as he is in the light, we have fellowship with one another, and the blood of Jesus, his Son, purifies us from all sin" (1 John 1:7).

9

The Unseen Battle

hristians who successfully work through transference commonly report engaging in some form of spiritual battle. Many struggle to save important relationships; some battle to retain their own sanity; a few fight to continue the ministry to which God has called them. I've heard many accounts from people who have persevered through this potentially debilitating dynamic.

Some have described the time leading up to the episode of transference: As it approached they felt that their mistaken perceptions of people had been supercharged by demonic suggestions that entered either directly into their minds or through the careless words of other people. Others expressed feelings of trudging through deep spiritual mud in their effort to press through their denial and name the problem as transference.

I've heard from some people who felt stymied at key points in their process of healing, such as when they were getting close to an accurate connection of past events with the present. Those in transference onto their spouses sensed an evil intent to bring harm to their whole family. And others, especially the ministers themselves, struggled with the fears that they would never regain their equilibrium so as to minister effectively once again.

In each case of successful resolution, however, those in transference were able to discern the spiritual battle and deal with it. They first exercised appropriate spiritual authority in personal prayer to fend off the unwelcome oppression. Then they learned to overcome each temptation as it came. And, finally, they chose to receive the truth as it was made evident to them.

In all these cases the winning combination also included the wider community whose earnest intercession and speaking of the truth were absolutely vital. These strategies, all working in concert, enabled the individuals to overcome the spiritual battle.

For Christians who persevere in this battle the rewards are manifold: They receive a God-given humility based on the full knowledge of their capacity for sin and evil, and they grow in discernment, especially as it relates to transference in their and others' souls. They may also experience a profound filling of healing grace to meet their deep needs. And they increase in strength and the ability to persevere.

Calling Evil Good

By contrast, those stuck in unresolved transferences suffer a constant state of demonic temptation. The consequences, especially over the course of time, cannot be overstated. Not only do they remain stuck in transference, either onto one person or several in serial, but their emotional, spiritual, intellectual, and moral growth slows down and can even grind to a halt.

Furthermore, they may eventually forfeit the good of their mind that has been transformed by the Holy Spirit. For in failing to deal with the transference they have left themselves open to the constant intrusion of demonic temptation. And, of course, the aim of the Evil One is not only to oppress the mind, but to take it over.

As Thomas à Kempis once wrote, "First there cometh to the mind a bare thought, then a strong imagination, afterward a delight, and evil motion, and then consent."[1] People consent when they receive into themselves the deluded and fearful thoughts that are suggested, incorporating them into their convictions about what is real.

They may become like those whom Isaiah described, "who call evil good and good evil, who put darkness for light and light for darkness" (Isaiah 5:20). This is a state of severest spiritual deception. Those in this condition end up out of touch with reality, isolated from other people, and estranged from God.

It is important to recognize that the dark spirits aim beyond simply oppressing the individual in transference, for they also seek to harm the surrounding community. When this involves people who are effectively serving together in ministry, such as the leaders of churches or Christian ministries, the spiritual battle aims to weaken or even destroy the kingdom work in which they are engaged. In these cases, unresolved transferences become more than simply a time-consuming pastoral concern but the avenue through which a fierce spiritual battle of great import and intensity descends.

Churches under Oppression

When transference occurs in the context of a Christian community it often becomes a public affair, even when a visible leader is not involved. When this happens it may seem as though a dark plague has descended on the church body. The people experience an upsurge of petty grievances, infighting, divisiveness, jealousy, envy, slander, and so forth. The immature and carnal impulses of those in transference seem to move from one to another like a virus. More deadly, however, is a church effectively forgetting their priority of worshiping God and fulfilling their mission. All of this reflects the spiritual battle enveloping the church.

Although not all spiritual battles involve transference, this dynamic seems to be a common manifestation of today's spiritual conflicts. But no universal cause-and-effect relationship exists between the two. For example, in some cases the unacknowledged transferences and the sins that typically accompany them serve as the open door through which the oppression enters a church body. In others, the proliferation of transference is preceded by the inroads of spiritual darkness from some other source.

And by contrast I have known of churches where the increase in transference indicated the Holy Spirit's work to purify the souls for greater ministry ahead. But regardless of the exact relationship between transference and spiritual battle in any given situation, the way through is always straightforward.

The first step is overcoming the widespread ignorance about this dynamic. The best place to begin is with education of the church leaders, both the lay leaders and staff. This should happen quietly and behind the scenes because an attempt to educate the congregation at large can backfire, being interpreted as an attempt to secure a wrong type of control over people.

Instead, the teaching should begin with those who are mature and already giving pastoral care to others. They are the ones who should be able to identify transference in themselves or others; they will need to be able to deal with it effectively.

Along with education is the need for special intercessory prayer. It seems that apart from divine intervention, these plagues of sin related to transference only grow more intense. For example, some transferences are so well hidden that only God can give the needed discernment. And his love and wisdom, which are bestowed on us as we seek him in prayer, are always needed to resolve them. To this end everyone involved should be called to diligent intercession.

Attacks on God's Servants

The spiritual battle is intensified when it involves Christian leaders. As clergy and directors of Christian ministries, their place of influence and potential to bless and advance the kingdom of God make them a worthwhile target for the Evil One. Thus effective leaders can experience an inordinate degree of spiritual battle in conjunction with being the object of others' transferences. At the very least their focus is diverted away from their vocation. In fact, the energy needed to deal with even one case of serious transference sometimes renders ministers all but incapable of fulfilling their responsibilities.

Those who have suffered in this way describe the surrounding spiritual battle in similar ways. For example, although many felt spiritually oppressed, emotionally depressed, or physically fatigued, they were unable to identify the source, especially if the transference was hidden. And when facing the accusations made against them, most were tempted to believe the very lies about themselves being touted by the one in transference.

After living for months or years under irrational and severe scrutiny, some leaders became overly self-conscious and fearful of offending people. Others reported the loss of relationships with friends, family, and ministry partners who had been stealthily drawn into the transference. A few struggled not to give way to discouragement and cynicism. And many entertained ways of retreating from completely fulfilling all that God had called them to do and to be, especially if they had fallen prey to bitterness over their suffering.

Some of the severest examples of spiritual battle that I have known of involve an element of unacknowledged transference onto Christian leaders, especially pathological transferences involving full-blown spiritual deception. Those transferring in these situations are so self-deceived that they believe they are doing the work of God by opposing valid ministries; they may even consider this their life's work.

These misguided ones tend to see danger where there is none. They mistrust trustworthy people while giving their allegiance to those who do not deserve it. They often call evil people good and good people evil. And because they have so little capacity to trust others, they eventually become completely isolated from any remaining friends or family. Nonetheless, such spiritually deceived people continue to carry on their work against God's servants, all the while claiming that they are true ministers of the gospel. The eternal consequences of such evil is known only to God.

Surviving such a spiritual battle, and pressing on to serve the Lord despite it, requires extraordinary wisdom. Sometimes it is possible to see the problem coming and to take precautions to avoid it, or at least to contain and manage it in such a way as to spare the ministries and leaders at risk. Pressing on through these types of transferences takes prayer, discernment, and dedication.

Dealing with this dynamic is almost always difficult and exhausting. It does, however, provide an opportunity for growth. As such these trials may well be the precursor to an increase in a community's depth and breadth of effectiveness in their advancement of the kingdom of God. Holding fast to such a hope helps leaders to persevere.

Those who survive the transference of others and those who overcome their own transference will find themselves made strong. They will be better able to face other difficulties in their lives and to run the race of faith to the finish.[2]

A Life of Prayer

Surviving transference and the surrounding spiritual battle can be a painful experience that nonetheless is redeemed by God. Opportunities for growth are imbedded in otherwise devastating circumstances and events.

It is always difficult, if not impossible, to determine the sources of our sufferings: Some are the consequences of our own actions; others result from Satan's ill intent for us; some are sent or allowed by God as a discipline. But whatever the reason for our trials, God is able to turn them into opportunities for our growth.

The Scriptures model a way of responding to difficulties that perceives God's purposes as accomplished through them. The first response is to give thanks for our difficulties because they can lead to the maturity that God desires in his people.

For example, the apostle James wrote, "My brothers and sisters, whenever you face trials of any kind, consider it nothing but joy, because you know that the testing of your faith produces endurance; and let endurance have its full effect, so that you may be mature and complete, lacking in nothing" (James 1:2–4, NRSV). This passage—along with the whole testimony of Scripture—indicates that the way to maturity is always forged in the fire of adversity.

The second response to strife is to ask God to purify the heart through the hardship. King David's psalms are peppered with such prayers: "Search me, O God, and know my heart; try me and know my anxious thoughts; and see if there be any hurtful way in me, and lead me in the everlasting way" (Psalm 139:23–24, NASB). And, "Surely you desire truth in the inner parts; you teach me wisdom in the inmost place. Cleanse me with hyssop, and I will be clean; wash me, and I will be whiter than snow" (Psalm 51:6–7).

The Lord hears and honors these prayers. In King David's life, for instance, such petitions were answered in the painful circumstances of his life wherein he gained, through humility before God, purity of heart. This illustrates the *holiness* that the Scriptures prescribe. And as it was for David, so it is for us: In answer to prayers for purity God allows difficult circumstances and spiritual battles in our lives that will press the heart to reveal its hidden contents. The humility and cleanness that result are foundational to Christian maturity.

When we give thanks to God in the midst of difficulty and battle, seeking inward purity, we will experience the light of the Holy Spirit searching our heart. Through God's illumination the broken areas in our lives can be cleansed, forgiven, healed, and strengthened. And it is not for our benefit alone, but for the blessing of our families and community if we will deal with our sins, the ways we have been sinned against, and the pressure of the Evil One.

PART

The Remedy

10

Dealing with Transference

O nce transference has been identified, it is critical to deal with the problem correctly. Those in transference have much to gain: If in humility they will face their sin, turn from it, and place themselves in a position to receive help, they can travel the road to great healing and fullness of life.

Toward Humbleness of Mind

Healing can ensue once those in transference acknowledge that this hidden dynamic has been at work. Such an admission requires humility, however, and when they lack this quality it is all but impossible for them to progress. More than any other sin, pride most often stands in the way of successfully resolving transferences.

The first step toward healing is for the one in transference to acknowledge that he has misjudged the object of his transference. To admit that one's perceptions and judgments have been faulty requires an uncommon humility—*humbleness of mind*, as it is sometimes translated in the New Testament.

The second step is for him to confess in humility that his attitudes or actions have been wrong. He must acknowledge the sinfulness of his *present* behavior and not shift the blame either onto the one against whom he has sinned or onto some person or event from the past. Almost always, those in transference need to be confronted by someone outside the situation who has objectivity.

It is uncanny, however, how obvious sinful behavior in an unacknowledged transference can be ignored by the surrounding community. Often as people become caught up in the needy one's railings against a certain individual, they overlook the fact of his gossip, slander, factiousness, and so forth. Somehow the one in transference succeeds in turning away all scrutiny from himself, onto the object of his hatred or envy. But if his sinful actions are confronted, he will then have more at stake in admitting his wrongdoing because he has drawn so many others into the deception. He must have great humility to take back the accusations.

The third step is for him to admit that he needs help in identifying and resolving the issues from the past from which spring the present confusion. This too requires humility because it means acknowledging that he is yet immature in some respect; his ways of thinking, feeling, and relating are still inordinately governed by the events and people that shaped his early life. It also requires humility because to acknowledge the failings of one's parents almost always points to the need to admit to one's own similar flaws.

"Choose Life"

Those in transference seem to be drowning in a quagmire of diseased feelings, thoughts, and reactions. In order to enact the steps toward the healing just described, they must *choose* to climb out of this pool of subjectivity and into union with Christ. Only in this union, as they put on the mind of Christ, will they find the objectivity they need to resolve the transference successfully.

Understanding the power of the will is the strongest key to helping a person come out of transference. Even in the severest cases, the human soul is able to choose the way of wellness.[1] This principle employs the biblical understanding of what it means to be human and departs from the classic psychoanalytic understanding of transference.

For Christians, the crisis of being confronted by the fact of transference denotes a watershed in the journey toward maturity. Transference brings out the worst in a person: All that is immature and unhealed in the soul rises to the surface. These elements threaten to take over the personality, overshadowing the real person created and renewed in God's image.

Once confronted, Christians in transference are at a crossroads. They either choose to acknowledge their sin and then keep on exercising their will as they work through the painful dynamic, or they deny it and hold fast to their illusions. To choose the latter is to settle for spiritual stagnation. For some it can even be the road to spiritual death.

Those who understand transference have the responsibility to exhort the needy ones to make the right choice in full view of the consequences. Such exhortation is modeled repeatedly in the Scriptures. For example, Moses had to impress upon the Israelites the far-reaching implications of the choices they were about to make in response to his call to turn from idolatry:

> See, I set before you today life and prosperity, death and destruction. For I command you today to love the LORD your God, to walk in his ways, and to keep his commands, decrees and laws; then you will live and increase, and the LORD your God will bless you in the land you are entering to possess.
>
> But if your heart turns away and you are not obedient, and if you are drawn away to bow down to other gods and worship them, I declare to you this day that you will certainly be destroyed.
>
> Deuteronomy 30:15–18

Like the Israelites who heard Moses' words, those in transference must choose: Will they confess their sins? Will they courageously deal with the pain of the past and turn their gaze away from the person they have made into an idol?

The lavish mercy of God—life and prosperity—await them if only they will choose to acknowledge their idolatry and the ways they have unjustly caused another to suffer. The deep knowledge that they need and have received mercy is important, because it makes it easier to extend forgiveness to those who wronged them in the past. In some cases the one they have transferred onto has reacted sinfully; this too they must forgive. But if instead they refuse to acknowledge their own sin or to forgive those who have injured them, they cut themselves off from God.

Setting Boundaries

Unfortunately, there are many examples of people in transference who will not respond to the exhortation of others. Instead they choose to cling to their sin and the delusion to which they have succumbed. In these cases, the people who surround those stuck in transference can help them most by setting appropriate boundaries around their behavior.

Those involved work together to determine what boundaries need to be set; they will seek to protect the object of the transference and to keep the unhealthy dynamic from spreading into the community. They then make these restrictions known to the one in transference and to any others who have been directly affected by the hurtful behavior. When done properly entire ministries can be spared, even if the one transferring refuses help.

Each case must be discerned separately, but certain actions are usually appropriate when setting boundaries in instances of unacknowledged transference:

- If the one transferring is making unreasonable demands on the object's time and attention, help him to understand the appropriate and expected ways to relate.
- Tell the one in transference which people are available to talk and pray with him.
- Ask him to take responsibility for any gossip, slander, and factiousness by refraining from these behaviors and making amends where possible. If the person is teachable, he will respond immediately and stop his sinful behavior. Oftentimes the insight he needs regarding his transference will then come easily.
- Request the secondary parties (those who have been taken in by the one in transference and who have passed on the delusion) to take responsibility for their gossip, slander, or

factiousness by ceasing from these behaviors and making restitution where possible.

- Inform the staff and lay leaders about the transference and instruct them how to uphold the boundaries.

An example of enacting restrictions around one in transference is the way that Cindy worked with the leaders in her church to discern what boundaries to set with me. Asking me not to write, visit, or call her were the needed parameters to protect Cindy from my bombarding her with my deluded accusations and demands. And equally important, not only did these limits help me check my sinful behavior, but they enabled me to realize what an idol I had made of Cindy and my friendship with her.

Limits to Factiousness

Another reason to set up strong boundaries is when the person in transference actively engages in factious behavior. Factiousness is lethal to the life of a church or ministry and therefore must be contained by erecting the right boundaries. In every case factious behavior must be confronted clearly and strongly, especially when leaders are involved.

An example of the way one governing body in a church minimized factiousness is a simple one. They let the people in their congregation know that they would not bring anonymous concerns or complaints to their meetings, but would attach names to any matters to be discussed. This policy was not meant to intimidate people into silence, but to weed out the influence of those who wished to stir up trouble.

Those with real discernment and wisdom, who would gladly take responsibility for expressing their concerns, felt more able to do so. At the same time the leaders were freed to focus on helping the church move forward in its mission, rather than spending their time managing complaints.

Sometimes the solutions to dealing with factiousness are not so easy. When warnings have been issued and the factious one is still not repentant, it is appropriate, according to the Scriptures, to ask her to leave the church. The apostle Paul has clear words of instruction for dealing with this particular sin:

> You must keep yourself entirely aloof from foolish disputes . . . from controversy, and from wranglings over the law. These are futile and of no benefit to anyone. As for a man who is given to factiousness, you may give him one warning and then another. If this remains unheeded, you should have nothing further to do with him, since you are well aware that this sort of man has a distorted mind, and has fallen into sin, and stands self-condemned.
>
> Titus 3:9–11, Cassirer

When factiousness is identified, the Scriptures make it plain that it must be confronted firmly. And furthermore, where there is no repentance there can be no fellowship. Unrepentant people are dangerous in a church for they will undermine the leadership, cast doubt on the ministry, and bring others into their spiritual deception. Paul says we are to have nothing more to do with such ones.

When a parting of ways is the only solution it is painful for a leader, for it often involves the loss of friendship and a reckoning with the fact that deep trust has been betrayed. More important, however, is rescuing the entire flock from danger through lovingly excommunicating the factious one. Sadly, when pastors wait too long to take this action the unrepentant person may not only leave of her own volition, but take others with her.

Dangerous Cases

Unresolved transferences can escalate into behavior that is dangerous—even criminal. Examples include stalking (following and watching the object of the transference), threatening to harm or kill family members, and making outlandish public declarations of love and devotion. Often this type of behavior is associated with those who belong in a mental hospital. Surprisingly, however, the instigators do not always look the part. They can be productive, well-respected members of the Christian community.

When these behaviors are observed, immediate action must be taken. Unfortunately, one of the first reactions is usually denial:

"This behavior is not normal for this person; it cannot be true." Or some make the mistake of naively trying to help the sick one by reasoning with him or offering psychological insight.

In reality, those who are involved in such severe behaviors are generally too mentally disturbed to receive ordinary encouragement and advice, much less to acknowledge their transference. Therefore the first priority is setting and enforcing firm, protective boundaries around the errant behavior for the safety of those involved.

A Newcomer—with a History

The way Pastor Miller and his fellow church leaders handled such a case provides a good example of how boundary-setting can contain and defuse a dangerous transference.

Pastor Miller, a skilled teacher and pastoral caregiver, was an associate pastor of a thriving church who was loved for his warm, fatherly manner. Because of these virtues, however, he attracted those who lacked affirmation from their fathers and who were inclined to transfer onto him.

John was a newcomer to the church and, unknown to all, had a history of transferences onto pastors. His pressing need was for assistance in finding a job and for support through his unemployment. As he made his situation known, he became acquainted with many leaders in the church, including Pastor Miller, the senior pastor, the church administrators, the worship leader, and some elders.

The speed by which he got to know so many of these leaders was an early indicator of his need for attention from authority figures. He told many of them that he was looking for a meaningful place to serve in the church and even expressed an interest in preparing for ordained ministry. Several on the pastoral staff, as well as a number of lay people, responded to his needs and found practical ways to help.

The staff member with whom John had the most contact was Pastor Miller, and it was to him that John confided his deeper need. He complained that he had frequently felt betrayed by others, including his wife and children, whom he was estranged from at the time. Pastor Miller quickly realized that John had difficulty in making and maintaining relationships of any kind.

As was typical of Pastor Miller, he was generous in the amount of time he gave to John, both in his office and over the phone. He made the mistake, however, of listening far too long to John's repetitious monologues about his unhappiness. He also underestimated the severity of John's problem.

Irrational Accusations; Chilling Behavior

Eventually Pastor Miller felt overwhelmed by the time and energy needed for this pastoral relationship. Thinking that John would respond well to ordinary pastoral care, he invited him to be part of a small group. Pastor Miller hoped this would be an opportunity for John to make new friends and to find another avenue for spiritual growth.

By way of preparing him to be a part of this group, Pastor Miller tried to help John become more aware of his immature ways of socializing that could make it difficult for him to fit in. For example, he gently prodded John toward more mature habits of communication, such as talking less and listening more. Initially John seemed to respond positively to the pastoral care and friendship. But before long, Pastor Miller was forced to confront John with a far more serious concern.

The problem came to light when John followed a woman to a Bible study that Pastor Miller happened to be visiting. The woman and the man she was with were extremely distraught when John appeared, and Pastor Miller gently requested that John leave the meeting. Later when the minister asked the couple about their fearfulness he learned that not only had John been stalking this woman for several weeks, but that he had threatened to kill the man only hours before the meeting.

Pastor Miller confronted John the next day and set the first boundary: John was not to attend the group again or to follow the woman. Having taken this action, Pastor Miller lost favor in John's eyes. The angry man accused him of betraying him, "just like everyone else he had ever trusted." When the pastor pointed out the irrationality of this accusation and reassured John of his desire to help him, it was to no avail. John was not open to hearing the truth.

Nonetheless, John's demands for Pastor Miller's attention continued. Finally the exasperated pastor explained that he would be unable to give more of his time to John. When he set up this personal boundary, John's anger intensified.

John then repeatedly tried to reach the pastor by phone. On one occasion he left a chilling message on Pastor Miller's answering machine: "Please repent, brother, or I'm . . . calling everybody in the church and letting them know the sinfulness of their assistant pastor. . . . I don't want it that way, but you've made it so."

Protective Boundaries

John could not carry out this threat, however, because the church leadership took decisive steps to defuse the situation. They had just recently discussed the implications of transference in a staff meeting and were all aware of the potentially harmful effects. Thus Pastor Miller had told the senior pastor about what was happening long before the situation became explosive. This successfully thwarted John's efforts to persuade the senior pastor to side with him against Pastor Miller. Also, as soon as Pastor Miller realized that there was a serious problem, he began to keep written notes of every conversation with John.

Upon the recommendation of the senior pastor, and with Pastor Miller's documentation in hand, the elders of the church held a meeting with John. Aware of their authority and responsibility to protect the church, they addressed John's threats and dangerous behavior. Without apology they informed him of the boundaries they had established: He was no longer allowed at church functions or on church property, nor could he contact any church member. They offered to reevaluate their decision if and when John fulfilled their stipulations to seek out psychological and social services (which he never did). John assented, and the elders wrote a letter to him that documented the agreement.

The elders also informed the local police of the problem with John. They concurred with the plan and agreed to remove John from the premises if he failed to keep the terms of the agreement.

Also, both Pastor Miller and the elders took care to protect the church from any possibility that John might instigate formal litigation. They kept written notes of every interaction with him.

On one occasion after the meeting with the elders, John appeared at a church service. When the elders informed him that they had already spoken to the police about his appearance he willingly left the premises and was not seen again.

Although Pastor Miller struggled at first with feeling that he had failed to help John, he eventually realized that John was not ready or willing to receive help. He also knew that he had taken the necessary action to protect himself, the church staff, and the congregation at large from real danger. Because he, along with the rest of the church leaders, understood the dynamic of transference it was possible to remedy the situation before it raged out of control.

Dealing with transference, as we have seen, is not always easy. Indeed, certain traps can ensnare us and keep us from a healthy resolution. We turn to these next.

11

Traps to Avoid

hen seeking to discern and deal with transference in a Christian setting, people make some common mistakes. This is not because they are nonprofessionals who are trying to employ a term from the psychological profession—although this may be a contributing factor. Rather they run into problems because naming transference involves discernment of sin and the frailties of the human soul.

As such, in certain instances transference may be mistaken for something else, or it could be discerned rightly but confronted poorly. Perhaps it is even misused so as to dismiss criticism of one's actual shortcomings. Despite the possibility of mistakes or abuse, however, pastoral caregivers need to feel free to name the problem for what it is and deal with it accordingly. To this end, several precautions can minimize the degree to which the term is misapplied.

Clothed with Humility

The first priority for anyone dealing with transference is to know one's own weaknesses. For example, a pastor may inadvertently and repeatedly draw to himself those most likely to transfer parental issues. He may then exercise the wrong kind of patience and thereby fail to name and contain the transference before it affects others in the church. In such a case the pastor must learn to receive insight from others who see him and the situation more objectively.

This calls for a rare and precious kind of humility—that which allows one to be open and honest with trusted others and to receive their counsel. The Scriptures indicate that the degree to which we receive God's grace depends on our humility not only before God, but also before one another: "All of you, clothe yourselves with humility *toward one another,* because, 'God opposes the proud but gives grace to the humble'" (1 Peter 5:5, emphasis mine).

It is this virtue—humility—that safeguards leaders from either mistakenly naming a problem as transference or failing to recognize their part in drawing those who will transfer onto them. Such humility, along with the friendship of those who are trustworthy, are gifts the Father longs to give his children.

Misusing the Term

The most obvious mistake to avoid is misnaming the problem. Several scenarios are typical in which this can happen. In some cases, for instance, people jump to wrong conclusions simply because they do not know enough about transference. The remedy for this error is for them to become more familiar with the signs of the dynamic and to make sure they are not basing their conclusion on just one or two indicators.

After such a mistaken experience, it is helpful and even vital for these individuals to share their concerns with someone who is trustworthy. For example, if a lay leader believes a certain person is in transference, she should share her thoughts with her minister to confirm or dismiss her hunch. Clergy also need input from other pastors or strong lay leaders before taking actions.

Similar is a second type of scenario, when a person understands transference but is prone to misjudgment and therefore may not investigate the matter sufficiently before proclaiming his so-called diagnosis. When this happens the surrounding community naturally resents him for taking on the self-appointed role of amateur psychoanalyst.

Sadly, rather than naming the dangerous lack of discernment, the community may thereafter be edgy when the word transference is mentioned. Thus they lose the benefit of dealing with this dynamic correctly.

The answer for the one who misjudges is greater humility. Beyond this he too needs to confer with others who can temper any tendency to hastily label other people's problems. And the community, of course, needs to be willing to confront and name the problem, rather than overlooking it out of a sentimentalized notion of love.

Third are those who misuse the term as a way to dismiss complaints that arise concerning themselves or other leaders. For example, a clergyman who actually does have a problem of needing to control others may dismiss the person who brings this issue to his attention. He may not only flatly reject the observation but insist that she is in transference. To do this discredits the individual by implying that her perceptions are not trustworthy. In such situations the careless use of the term serves to mask the real problems.

And finally, some mistakenly name as transference the inevitable bumps that accompany growing relationships, which are actually just ordinary difficulties in relating. This error results largely from not only a lack of understanding about transference but also comprehension of the way relationships are built. For example, when a relationship evolves from merely an acquaintance to a friendship certain misperceptions will need to be worked through.

Similarly, to some degree all people project their own emotions and past experiences into present relationships. For instance, a woman who has suffered a miscarried pregnancy will have a good idea of how another woman in the same situation might feel. As such, this kind of projection is the basis of empathy, which is vital to real relating and has nothing to do with transference. By contrast, the kind of misperceptions and projections that go along with transference serve to block and destroy a relationship rather than facilitate it.

Isolation or Escape

As we saw in the cases above, pastoral caregivers must seek fellowship with discerning peers if they are to avoid the traps of misnaming transference. They also need this support to keep from being crushed if they do become the focus of another's transference.

For example, when a Christian leader becomes the recipient of another's diseased feelings and emotions, she desperately needs the wise and knowledgeable counsel and prayer of others. If she does not already belong to a prayer group, it may be too late to gather one for this purpose. Without being upheld by others, she is prone to such mistakes as confiding in the wrong people (those who have been taken in by the transference), isolating herself, or running away from the situation altogether.

For a circle of Christian friends to support one of their members who is receiving a transference, they must know and trust one another well enough to discuss the accusations and concerns openly. They will readily see when an allegation is ridiculous and can be dismissed. Likewise, they will realize when an accusation is based on a person's real area of weakness that needs to be strengthened. Also, they will be familiar enough with each other's personal histories so as to recognize patterns of subjective or sinful reactions. Finally, they will trust one another enough to receive personal prayer and give wise counsel to each other.

In such a group the members can direct prayer in specific ways for the one who has become the object of transference. For example, once it is discerned that a demonic oppression is present, the prayer partners can exercise their spiritual authority to put the dark presence to flight. Such a prayer can be as simple as, "Lord, in the Holy Name of Jesus, we ask you to lift this darkness from her body, her mind, and her spirit. Come now, Holy Spirit, and fill her with your light, your truth, and your love."[1] Similarly, the group can ask the Lord to release the person spiritually and physically from any effects of the sins committed against her such as slander, envy, gossip, and the like.

Also, if the object of the transference has reacted sinfully, others in the group can lead her to confess her wrong response. Likewise they can lead her to extend forgiveness toward the one in transference and to any others who have been taken in by it. And finally, any words of encouragement or wisdom from the Scriptures that come up during prayer can be written down so that the person may refer back to them as she waits upon the Lord for the problem's full resolution.

The Limitations of Therapy

When confronted with transference, some immediately shy away from the related difficulties and recommend that the needy person seek the expert help of a professional therapist. But apart from the illumination of the Holy Spirit and an in-depth understanding of the dynamics of transference, even good counselors and psychologists fumble in their attempts to recognize, interpret, and resolve transferences. This is especially true as related to relationships outside that of the client and therapist.

Therapists are trained with regard to transference almost exclusively in terms of the client-therapist relationship. Therefore, most counselors are not on the lookout for the transference dynamic when it occurs in their client's other relationships. And when it does, they are limited to their client's reporting of the situation and cannot test the reality of those perceptions by talking to the other person. This is in contrast to when the therapist as the object of the transference can, therefore, validate or invalidate the client's perceptions.

Another reason why therapists are limited in their ability to help a person resolve a transference is that they are not trained to address the moral and spiritual aspects of transference. Instead, they are prepared to deal with transference as a real but morally neutral dynamic in the therapeutic process. They are not prepared to help a client discern, name, and repent of the sins of the heart such as envy, bitterness, malice, and so forth.

Unless a therapist knows how—and has the freedom professionally—to invite the presence of God into the therapeutic process, it will not happen in the context of professional counseling. The responsibility then rests on the individual to enter into a vital, personal relationship with God wherein he or she can receive illumination and find the grace to repent and to forgive those people and circumstances that have energized the transference.

Given therapists' limitations in dealing with transference outside the professional milieu, not to mention the scarceness of gifted Christian therapists, people naturally look for help within their established relationships, including the person who has become the object of their transference. But most marriages, pastoral relationships, employer-employee relationships, and friendships cannot withstand the confusion and oftentimes spiritual oppression brought on by the transference dynamic. In these cases a skillful therapist or pastoral counselor who understands transference is needed to help the person sort out the past from the present and to relieve the strain on current relationships.

Pastoral counselors, professional and lay, can be helpful to a person in transference. But they must know their limitations and keep the right boundaries intact. For example, they must be careful not to set up a situation wherein they try to unravel the mysteries of another's soul or become a substitute parent to fill all the losses from the past. Nor can they try to make use of the transference in the same way a therapist would, but instead need to point the person to the resources of the cross. Only there will the needy individual gain the courage to face the past as it really was, to forgive, to grieve, and to walk in the freedom of God.

Dangerous Subjective Reactions

In many cases, such as my own, transference is truly one-sided. But in other situations a person will elicit countertransference and subjective reactions in the object of the transference. To understand what countertransference looks like outside a therapeutic setting, it is helpful to see how it occurs inside this milieu. A good example of this dynamic is the case of Kirk, a professional counselor, and his client Mary.

Misunderstandings and Confusion

Having been referred to Kirk by a social service agency, Mary arranged to come in for her first appointment and fill out the necessary paperwork. But having misunderstood when she was to arrive, she was still completing the forms when the counseling appointment was scheduled to begin. In addition, the clerical staff had misplaced her background files. Consequently she missed her first session, and so began a series of frustrations between Mary and Kirk.

Their rescheduled appointment took place a week later. As it began, Mary revisited her angry feelings of the previous week. After Kirk explained and apologized, Mary began to complain about her problems with the county health department in securing services for her handicapped son.

Kirk tried to help her understand the policies of this agency and sought to encourage her not to take their slowness so personally. But when he did this Mary accused him of conspiring with the county health department to keep her from getting the help she needed for her son.

Kirk then calmly asked her to explain her conspiracy theory. Instead of doing so Mary attacked him, calling into question his competence as a therapist. She also threatened legal action. Kirk was caught off guard and angrily defended himself. An argument ensued, the session ran thirty minutes over, and finally Kirk demanded that the woman leave his office.

Avoiding Unwise Love and Hate

Many hours later Kirk was still angry, and in his mind he rehashed the argument again and again. After a nearly sleepless night, he eventually realized that the incident had tapped into deep, unresolved anger from his own past. Having been trained in the dynamics of such situations, Kirk knew his anger was part of a countertransference reaction onto Mary.

A few days later he discussed the situation with his supervisor and then humbly and simply apologized to Mary for letting his anger get out of control. He did not mention the way his response related to his own past issues.

Over the course of several months Mary was able to work through her transference onto Kirk and deal with her generalized paranoia toward social service agencies. And although Kirk sometimes had to check his subjective reactions to her irrational attacks, he was able to avoid countertransference. Had Kirk been unable to overcome his subjective responses, he could have referred Mary to another therapist.

Frank Lake has written of the danger of countertransference when one is working with paranoid persons like Kirk's client:

> At times the pastor will be forced into loving this needy child, at others into hating this hateful child. Unless the pastor has super-human virtue he will both love and hate unwisely and too well. The parishioner's confusion will remain, for few of us dare be both loving and honest under the devastating attacks of paranoid suspicion and inquisition.[2]

In Kirk's case he was loving and honest, yet he skillfully avoided giving Mary further ammunition for her paranoid accusations against him.

Seeking Help in Painful Situations

Countertransference such as this therapist experienced happens in pastoral care situations as well and is a danger to be avoided. But when it does occur, the person in countertransference needs as much help as the one in transference. The one receiving the transference may be suffering from the eruption of her own repressed emotions and memories that she cannot deal with by herself. In fact, the stress of being the object of a strong transference can lead to physical and emotional breakdowns.

More common, however, are certain simple subjective reactions by the object of a transference that serve to complicate and exacerbate the situation. For example, a pastor of a large congregation had been desperately trying to handle unjust accusations brought against him. After some months he hired a costly conflict-resolution specialist to listen to both sides and facilitate resolution.

Upon hearing about the specialist, a woman in the congregation insinuated to the pastor that his motives for hiring the expert were self-serving. He reacted by vociferously expressing his anger over the no-win situation her accusation put him in. His anger had nothing to do with his past personal history; it was an honest response to an extremely frustrating and painful present situation. Unfortunately those making a case against him witnessed his outburst and added it to their list of grievances.

It is important, therefore, for the objects of a transference to learn to keep subjective reactions in check. Although they desperately need to vent their frustration, they must be exceptionally careful about when and where this happens.

Prideful Peacemakers

Those who work alongside and support the ministry of Christian leaders face great challenges and temptations with regard to transference. When, for example, a leader is on the receiving end of a transference, one working for him might be tempted to engage pridefully in the role of a peacemaker. He might endeavor to get the two parties to talk to one another or he may secretly go back and forth between them in seeking a resolution.

In taking on this new role he overestimates his capacity to limit the destructive power of a serious transference. His attempts will flounder. Commonly he will get sucked into the litigious, irrational claims of the one in transference and thereby come under the same cloud of oppression.

Once confronted with the fact that he has become part of the problem he has important choices to make: Will he honestly face the ways in which someone else's transference has hooked into his own unresolved issues? Will he confess his pride in attempting to be a peacemaker and acknowledge that he has made matters worse? Will he shake off any demonic interference or the misinformation and slander of others?

Like the one in transference, this person must *choose* to believe what is true, resisting any inclination to spiritual and intellectual sloth. If he loses the battle for truth in his own mind or fails to overcome his pride, he too will fall into spiritual deception.

Quite often certain signs are apparent when such a person is struggling with irrational thoughts regarding the leader he is called to walk alongside. For example, he may be fearful that he is lending his efforts to a "controversial" ministry, even though if asked he would admit that this is illogical. Or he may pull back from full involvement in the ministry because he has internalized the paranoia of those in transference.

Similarly, this person may cease relating personally to the leader, again because he has taken in irrational fears. Or he may distance himself from the ministry because he is intimidated by the strain of spiritual battle and the responsibility to stand in the truth. When he gives in to irrational fears in any of these ways, the work suffers, he leaves a gap in the ministry team, and the leader is left with one fewer ally.

The solution for the person who realizes that he has come under the oppressive cloud of another's transference is first to admit it in humility. After calling on the Holy Spirit, the Spirit of truth, he can prayerfully and painstakingly write out the process by which he became ensnared, including his attitudes and behavior.

Where he has sinned, he should confess this to the Lord as specifically as possible. Eventually he may need to share what he has written with someone who understands transference and can help him gain greater objectivity. Also, he likely will need prayer for the release of any spiritual oppression. Finally, he must obey any direction the Lord gives him for making right his relationship to the leader with whom he works.

By contrast, such a person can also be vitally important in helping a leader in such circumstances. He may, for example, see the transference building up before it erupts and thus make it possible to defuse the situation. He may also be able to warn others who are in danger of becoming involved. Finally, he may be able to suggest to the leader ways of steering clear of other potential transferences.

Sinful Shepherds

Sometimes ministers are the ones transferring onto others. Because their position lends them power and authority, their transferences will often go unchallenged. Obviously this is extraordinarily harmful to the person who is the object of the transference, who often is compelled to leave the church. But it also places the pastor and the church in a perilous place of spiritual danger.

Perhaps the most common scenario of this occurrence happens when male pastors transfer onto women in their congregations. These transferences often follow a similar pattern. At first, during the phase of positive transference, the pastor idealizes the woman. He might encourage her forward in leadership in the church, even if she is not ready. If his idealization becomes erotic he will be dangerously vulnerable to sexual temptation, even to the point of sexual aggression. And when such a man is married his wife will soon pale in comparison to the woman he has idealized, whether or not his transference has a sexual expression.

Then, as the transference turns negative, his sentiments toward the object of his transference will flip-flop and he will become hypercritical of the woman. In extreme cases he may attack her publicly and drive her from the church. She, of course, is left feeling confused, rejected, and humiliated. Unless the pastor realizes what has happened, he may soon find another woman to idealize and the cycle will begin again. Obviously, this dynamic can occur in many different contexts other than churches.

Like anyone in transference, a pastor will, to some extent, lose his grip on what is real. This negatively affects his capacity to teach and preach, to give pastoral care, and to provide leadership to the church. His unconfessed sin gives license to others and leaves the church vulnerable to increased spiritual battle. Obviously, he is in danger of discrediting and disgracing his own ministry.

As we have seen, there are many traps to avoid related to confronting transference in others. But perhaps as you have been reading you have the sinking feeling that *you* are the one in transference. Naming this dynamic is the first step to freedom, which, along with the other steps, we look at next.

12

What to Do if It's You

If you suspect that you are suffering under the weight of some hot, furry clothing, you can take several practical steps to shed the stifling garments and walk in the freedom of a child of God. The first, of course, is to have a measure of certainty that indeed you have been transferring onto another. The willingness to admit this, even though it may seem shameful or discouraging, is strong evidence of being well on the way toward healing. By contrast, those who adamantly refuse to consider this possibility are the furthest from getting help.

The following list of questions will help if you are unsure whether you are in transference. If you answer yes to many of the following questions your uncertainty should be cleared up. It's important to emphasize that the questions focus on how *frequently* these behaviors appear. Some relational dynamics apparent in unhealthy transferences can also be present to a much lesser degree in healthy relationships, although obviously not the sinful, litigious, slanderous ones.

- Are my thoughts preoccupied with a specific person or situation? Have I lost sleep thinking about him or her? Do I feel drained of energy for other important concerns because I am so otherwise absorbed?

- Do I frequently hold imaginary conversations in my mind with the person who may be the object of my transference?
- Do I often find myself telling others about my relationship with this person, whether by way of praising him idealistically or by venting criticism?
- When I think of this person, do I frequently struggle with envy or jealousy?
- Do I often wonder about what this person is thinking or feeling about me? Have I discovered later that these notions were far from the truth?
- Is my concentration in prayer frequently broken by thoughts about this person?
- Am I praying almost exclusively for him?
- Am I judging her as I read the Scriptures, applying verses to her?
- Do I have childish expectations of him or have outbursts of tantrum-like anger? Am I regressing into childishness in other areas of my life as well?
- Do I sense an increased amount of spiritual oppression?
- Is there a strong unreal quality about my perceptions of this person?
- Have I frequently engaged in gossip about this person to others?
- Do I often overreact to small offenses from this person? Or have I imagined wrongs when they were not there? Or were unintentional?
- Does this person find my need to talk to or spend time with him overwhelming? Is my relationship with her consuming so much of my time that I cannot attend to other important responsibilities or relationships?

When we are just beginning to acknowledge a transference, the help of others is crucial. Trusted individuals should confirm or dismiss our appraisal of the situation and then help us avoid lapsing back into denial or giving up in despair or depression. We will then need objective, and sometimes even directive, input from another in order to get unstuck.

Actually, the speed with which the transference can be resolved is facilitated when we simply open up our heart to someone else. Somehow sharing the burden serves to weaken the power of the delusion—and any accompanying demonic oppression—that may threaten to take over our rational abilities.

Repenting and Renouncing

If we have concluded that we are in the grips of transference, a good place to begin the healing process is with confession and repentance, so as to open the resources of Christ's redeeming work on the cross. The first thing to confess is any idolatry toward the person who is the object of the transference. Specifically, we must acknowledge the ways that we have desired or even demanded that this person meet the needs that only God can fulfill.

For example, when a woman looks to another human being to make up for a deep deprivation she suffered in infancy, she needs to confess the idolatry of looking to a person to provide something that can only come from God's healing touch. A man with this same need might have to confess his demands of his wife to take care of him as though he were a small child and she his mother.

Similarly, we may need to acknowledge the ways that we have looked to a certain individual to meet needs that belong to the domain of another relationship. For example, a woman might have to repent for expecting her pastor to affirm her in ways that only her father could, or for seeking a kind of intimacy with him that only her husband can provide appropriately. In confessing and turning away from these wrong desires she aligns herself with God's ordering of relationships as revealed in the Scriptures. She also lays aside her mistaken ideas of relating and the stubborn rebellion that insists on having legitimate needs met through inappropriate means.

Along with repenting of idolatry, we need to confess any other sin that has erupted from the transference, such as gossip, slander, malice, foolish talk, inordinate anger, jealousy, envy, and so forth. After confessing these transgressions to God and receiving his forgiveness, we may also need to ask the forgiveness of those whom we have hurt. Then, finally, as the source of the transference comes to light, we should confess the ways we have wrongly reacted to the difficult circumstances, suffering, or the sins of others against us.

For example, I knew of a man who had an inadequate bond with his mother in infancy and who had reacted to the birth of his baby brother with strong jealousy. He had also indulged in jealous and envious emotions toward other men all his life. As his history came to light in his transference onto a colleague, he had to confess his sinful reaction that began in infancy and continued throughout his life. After taking responsibility for his reactions in the past and confessing his shortcomings in the present, he received forgiveness from the Lord. He was then able to extend forgiveness to his mother.

Quieting the Mind

When coming out of transference we have a battle to fight and win with our patterns and habits of thought. As long as we continue to focus our minds on the person of our transference, we will not make significant progress. Therefore we must begin by acknowledging that we have effectively "practiced the presence" of a person rather than of God. By this I mean that we have centered our hearts and minds on another person rather than God.

From then on we need to accept our responsibility to choose, through an act of the will, what we will think about. For example, each time we find ourselves holding an imaginary conversation with another, or when we realize that we are litigiously reviewing their actions, we simply stop our train of thought. Then we turn the eyes of our heart toward God and confess our diseased thought patterns. We then can focus our minds and hearts on God.

At this point it is also helpful for us to do a mental reality check. For example, we might ask ourselves the questions, "Where am I? What should I be doing at this moment?" Having answered these questions we can focus our attention back to the situation at hand and away from the fanciful world of our obsessive thoughts.

When learning to control the patterns of my thinking, at many times I felt it was all but impossible. In these moments I recalled the apostle Paul's words in 2 Corinthians 10:5: "We destroy arguments and every proud obstacle to the knowledge of God, and take every thought captive to obey Christ" (RSV). Paul may not have been dealing with my problem, but he understood the need for Christ's dominion to extend even into the arena of a person's thoughts.

When I felt helpless against the tempest in my mind, I would desperately, but confidently, ask the Lord to quiet it. For surely the Son of God who calmed the waters of a stormy sea could speak his peace to my troubled thoughts. And he never failed to send his Holy Spirit in answer to this prayer. Moreover, the light of God seemed to accompany these experiences of supernatural peace, giving me more insight into the real source of my need.

If we are struggling with unhealthy thought patterns, we do not seek merely to extinguish our painful thoughts, as though they were nothing more than a fire to be put out. Instead, our way of thinking and feeling needs to be healed and renewed. To my knowledge, the best way to do this is through keeping a prayer journal.[1]

We begin by inviting the Lord to be present, and we ask him to help us write out our thoughts and feelings honestly. And then with a Bible nearby, we put down in our journal the recurrent themes of our thoughts, fears, fantasies, and so forth. This serves several purposes: It helps to untangle confused thoughts, makes plain the emotions that are involved, and provides a record that will help us avoid slipping back into denial.

This process also enables us to step back and see our thoughts more objectively. For example, we may even be able to laugh at how ridiculous some of our notions are. Or we may finally begin to grieve over the pain we see in our written account. Or perhaps we will realize what danger we have been in and seek out professional, and even psychiatric, help.

Finally, we listen for the words of the Lord, either through the Scriptures or the still, small voice of the Holy Spirit, and write these in our journal as well. Specifically, we ask the Lord to search out and heal those wounded areas from which the transference springs.

In response, the Lord sends his insight into the problems at the crux of the transference, helping us make the needed connections between the past and the present. He gives us the wonderful gift of conviction of sin to illumine what we may have overlooked, to validate the ways in which we have been hurt, and to point to the need to extend forgiveness. And he ministers his tender, healing balm and gives us the encouraging words we need. Finally, he sends his wisdom as to what we should do next.

Taking Authority over Oppression

The influence of dark spiritual powers in transference, though it should not be skipped over, is not difficult to deal with once we discern its presence. For if we have renounced any known idolatry and the sins associated with transference, we can then freely exercise our spiritual authority to banish this influence from our minds. Doing so helps us overcome the problem of troubling or obsessive thoughts that may have been interjected by spiritual sources. Once the strain of the demonic influence is relieved, we can more easily deal with our own confused thoughts.

As we proceed through the process of resolving transference we must grow in our capacity to perceive when we are being tempted by the Evil One. I have noted three common patterns of temptation. First are the alluring suggestions to regress into old patterns of defense against inner pain. For example, a person who was once addicted to something, chemical or otherwise, may be tempted to engage in that behavior again.

The second form of temptation is to reintroduce into the mind, either directly or through the words of another person, the very same obsessive thoughts that we have just fought hard to overcome. And the third is the temptation to despair, giving up hope in God's power to heal and in our capacity to persevere.

Thankfully, God promises to come to the aid of those who seek him in the midst of temptation: "Submit yourselves, then, to God.

Resist the devil, and he will flee from you. Come near to God and he will come near to you" (James 4:7–8).

We can recognize temptation in two simple ways. The first is to perceive the telltale characteristics of thoughts that are in line with the personality and activity of Satan as described in the Scriptures. For instance, they are accusing toward the self or others, fear-inspiring, despairing, destructive, vengeful, unloving, and so forth.

The second is to learn to recognize when we are most vulnerable to temptation. Although it may seem to come out of the blue, the timing of temptation most often follows a diabolical pattern. It may come when we are most weak and vulnerable. Or it may appear at a strategic time, such as when we are on the verge of a personal breakthrough or when we are moving forward to serve the Lord. The goal, then, is to recognize and resist temptation when it comes, rather than allowing it a home in our hearts.

Committing to Persevere

We must acknowledge that transference takes time to work through. I have observed that people tend to spend between six and eighteen months in the process. During this time they can count on experiencing a great deal of pain—usually the hurt and anguish they have been running from for a lifetime. But at the end of the road lies a great reward, and what is needed to realize this is a generous amount of perseverance.

This perseverance comes as we set our wills to cooperate with the Lord in every way, crying out to him for the strength we need. The Lord has an impeccable track record of answering prayers for strength, as the psalmist testified: "I sought the LORD, and he answered me, and delivered me from all my fears. Look to him, and be radiant; so your faces shall never be ashamed. This poor man cried, and the LORD heard him, and saved him out of all his troubles" (Psalm 34:4–6, RSV).

Our strength is also renewed as we faithfully participate in a worshiping community. At times this can be difficult if we tend to isolate ourselves from others when we are hurting; this is especially true if our transferences involve fears of trusting others. If so, we must choose to act in a way that is contrary to how we feel.

For example, we must simply decide to go to church, a small group, or an appointment with our pastor even when we dread doing so. We must also keep up our personal relationships as much as possible, taking advantage of ordinary opportunities for healthy relating to others. It also helps to have an outlet for being outwardly directed.

While I was working through my transference onto Cindy, for instance, it was good to stay busy helping others when working at the soup kitchen. This activity served to provide a temporary and wholesome distraction from my suffering, allowing me to replenish my spiritual and emotional energies.

It can also be helpful, and sometimes is absolutely essential, to have ongoing help from a counselor. This provides the needed accountability to keep working on the painful issues, and it can also be the source of important insight. Some counselors can work in conjunction with our efforts to journal and pray our way through the problem.

Finally, a counselor can monitor any depression, anxiety, and so forth that might call for medical attention. Such medical help is commonly needed when one finally is able to slough off the transference and discover the underlying issues.

Removing any furry costume we may have acquired takes time, prayer, humility, and the help of others. But once we are free to stand as the sons and daughters of God, we will never again want to don those false and constraining garments.

A Happy Ending

*A*s we have seen in the preceding chapters, transference can occur naturally and frequently in any situation where people work or live closely together. Because of the widespread ignorance about this powerful dynamic, many, if not most, of these situations have endings that at best are unhappy, and at worst are disastrous and diabolical. But as my story demonstrates, it is possible to have the happiest and most meaningful resolution as well.

In concluding this book it is fitting to tell another story of the way a person's fundamental choice to look fully to God for her healing, coupled with a basic understanding of the dynamic of transference, led to a successful resolution and to extraordinary personal growth. This is beautifully shown in the story of two of my colleagues.

An Idealized Image

Ita's friendship with Mario began after his graduation from seminary when he moved to a town near hers. Prior to this, she had interacted with him briefly through mutual friends as well as attending Pastoral Care Ministry schools where he was ministering.

When she learned he was moving into the area, Ita offered to help him organize his move and to store some of his furniture in her home. She did whatever she could to make him feel welcome, such as introducing him to her social circles in the church.

Several months later, Mario asked Ita to be a small-group leader in his ministry to help Christians overcome difficulties related to sexuality. She happily agreed and graciously offered to hold the meetings in her home.

Initially Ita found Mario to be a warm, witty, strong, and healthy man. The more she interacted with him, the more she was attracted to him. Her trust in and admiration for him grew even deeper as she watched him at work as a pastor.

Before long, Ita found herself sizing Mario up as a potential husband, thinking, "This could work." In retrospect, she realized that even then she was in the positive stage of transference, having superidealized Mario from the earliest point in their friendship.

Prior to this time, Ita had been in therapy for several years dealing with issues related to her family of origin that had resulted in a pattern of emotional dependency on women. Up until this point, she had by her own evaluation been too unstable to consider marriage. But now things had changed: She was well-established in her church community, she had several good friendships, she had a stable job, and she owned her own home. Her emerging hopes for marriage seemed to her a milestone in her healing.

But during this period of stability, and even as she was warming to the idea of marriage, Ita began to come in touch with inexplicable anger and mistrust toward men. Immediately, however, strong subconscious defenses in her soul started to work against her dealing with these painful matters.

For example, Ita began to battle with deep waves of suicidal depression along with brief flashbacks of long repressed memories. She did not know where these emotions were coming from but realized that they stood in the way of her achieving her dream to get married. So at a church service on New Year's Eve she prayed, "Lord, whatever it takes, I want you to help me get ready to be married." With this prayer she effectively gave the Lord permission to help her discover and overcome the root of her depression.

A Dark Obsession

By the time Ita prayed this prayer, even though she had not expressed it to anyone or even admitted it to herself, she had set her hopes for marriage primarily on Mario. But her desires became unmistakably apparent when Mario asked one of her best friends, Nancy, on a date. Ita reacted with anger toward them both, soon displaying intense envy and jealousy. While in the midst of this carnal response, she appeared to others as set on capturing Mario's sole attention and demanding exclusive rights to Nancy's friendship.

Obviously, Ita reacted far more intensely than the normal anger or disappointment over unrequited love. She was flooded with emotions that were rooted in a deep wound in her soul—something unrelated to Mario. She continued to experience flashbacks and was plagued with suicidal fantasies. Like many in transference, at times she thought she would rather die than face the root of her problem.

As Mario continued to date Nancy, Ita's appraisal of Mario shifted radically. Rather than widely praising his virtuous qualities as before, she became hypercritical of him. Like anyone in transference, she was deeply confused as her current thoughts about Mario blurred together with her resurfaced feelings from the past.

With mind set in high gear, she severely and litigiously scrutinized Mario's ministry and relationships. Eventually she drew others into her efforts to defame him. She seemed determined to prove to everyone that Mario was not the good and godly man he appeared to be. In her obsession she moved further and further away from dealing with her real problem.

At the same time, Ita found it increasingly difficult to relate to her friends. She often felt strangely let down, betrayed, and abandoned. Even though she knew these feelings were irrational and not based on anything her friends had done, she quickly regressed into old habits of isolating herself and making it difficult for her friends to contact her. She simply did not know how to let them into her suffering.

As Ita's depression deepened her chief temptation was to run away, leaving her church family, her home, and everything. She felt disconnected from reality and from those around her, and she dreamed about moving someplace far away from there.

The situation, which had been building for about three months, climaxed on the weekend before Mario's ordination into the priesthood. On the Sunday prior to the event Ita stayed home from church. Knowing that all her friends would be out, she left messages on their answering machines and notes on their car windshields. In each message she expressed her anger and self-pity and proclaimed that she was leaving the church.

Inviting Christ In

All along, Mario knew that Ita was in transference and had been praying about when and how to confront her. Having discussed the problem with his prayer cell and the staff of the church, he had their full support. When he heard of her behavior on that Sunday, he knew the time was right to meet with her.

Mario asked a woman on the church staff, whom Ita knew and trusted, to join him in this meeting; together they helped Ita to understand that she was in transference. They challenged her not to run but to stay in relationship with both of them, promising her that if she would work through the transference, they would help her. They also assured her that Christ would walk with her through the broken places in her soul. In doing so they did exactly what was needed to help Ita.

During that meeting Ita distinctly remembers consciously choosing to trust them, to accept their assessment of the problem, and to put her trust fully in the Lord. Before leaving the office she enjoyed the first glimmer of relief from her suffering and the hope for good things to come.

In the weeks and months that followed, Ita was able to turn her focus away from Mario so that she could squarely face the real source of her pain. Pride and self-pity stood in the way of her admitting that even after many years of effort, she was still dealing with unresolved issues from the past. She was disheartened to realize how many sinful patterns she still had to confess. But she overcame her pride and discouragement, and with the help of her therapist she came to the root of her misery.

Eventually she faced the worst of her memories and invited Christ into them. She was thereby enabled to forgive the "unforgivable." While doing so her grief and depression deepened and her emotional anguish became actual physical pain. Then, as odd circumstance would have it and by no fault of her own, she lost her job. She truly hit bottom. And in that place of darkness she found that she could be certain of only the most elemental realities: Her pain was real, God was real, and "God is with me at the bottom."

In remembering her story Ita recalls coming to a moment when, in her words, she "stopped fighting." Even if this paralyzing depression never lifted, she determined that she would love and worship God. This key relinquishment, seemingly so ironical, marked a turning point in her recovery. With it she started to emerge from the depression.

It took several months for the depression to dissipate entirely and for her to regain hold on what was objective and true about Mario and others. She had to work painstakingly through her anger toward men that issued out of her childhood and her Asian heritage. But eventually, about seven months after the transference first turned negative, Ita remembers one day realizing, "It is over. I am through the transference."

Thereafter she was not only free from serious depression but she rapidly matured to the point of coming into her own ministry in Christ. She also found new strength in her capacity to carry on healthy relationships. Some months later she met Bob, the man she was to marry. In his love she quickly blossomed and, just as she had prayed, she was soon ready to be his wife.

Grace upon Grace

> Surely our griefs He Himself bore,
> And our sorrows He carried. . . .
> He was pierced through for our transgressions,
> He was crushed for our iniquities;
> The chastening for our well-being fell upon Him,
> And by His scourging we are healed.
>
> Isaiah 53:4–5, NASB

Transference can be a doorway through which Jesus enters our souls to bring healing where we require it most. Prior to such an experience we may be unaware of our great need for Jesus to enter certain subterranean chambers of our hearts.

Thus, inasmuch as he is yet uninvited, Jesus stands outside the door of these deep places in our hearts. The crisis of transference, however, can serve to awaken us to hear him patiently calling, basin and towel in hand, as he awaits an invitation into the heart's darkened chambers where his healing and cleansing are required.

The Lord begins his work the very instant that we welcome him in and he illumines, cleanses, and rearranges the disordered rooms in our souls. As he does this work he invites us to surrender every grievous loss, sorrowful disappointment, and bitter offense to him, and to confess every known sin. Then, even as Isaiah foresaw, Jesus lovingly responds to our contrition by generously pouring out his healing and well-being.

We then can take to heart the apostle Peter's words: "If, then, through your submission to the truth your souls have been made pure so as to engender in you an unfeigned love, let the love you bear one another be one that comes from the heart and is ever fervent" (1 Peter 1:22, Cassirer).

As Peter says, those whose hearts have been purified through submission to the truth (as it is in the furnace of transference) are dramatically emboldened to love others. Thus they are set free to love their family, friends, and all whose lives intertwine with their own.

A person's choice, then, to trust, love, and obey God completely in the midst of transference releases great and eternal benefits to whole families and Christian communities. Herein God demonstrates his power to transform and triumph over all that is evil, fallen, and broken in the individual soul.

To participate in this outworking of Christ's victory is to experience abundant, transforming grace, even as the apostle John described: "Out of his fullness we have, all of us, received grace upon grace. For while the law was given through Moses, truth and grace have come through Jesus Christ" (John 1:16–17, Cassirer).

The manifold blessings that can be ours in the midst of transference come to us as we place our hope completely in the Lord. We express our faith and hope through bold petition to the triune God for the help that we need. A wonderful place to begin is with these beautiful prayers from the Anglican prayer book:

> O God, you declare your almighty power chiefly in showing mercy and pity: Grant us the fullness of your grace, that we, running to obtain your promises, may become partakers of your heavenly treasure; through Jesus Christ our Lord, who lives and reigns with you and the Holy Spirit, one God, for ever and ever. Amen.[1]

> O God, whose blessed Son came into the world that he might destroy the works of the devil and make us children of God and heirs of eternal life: Grant that, having this hope, we may purify ourselves as he is pure; that, when he comes again with power and great glory, we may be made like him in his eternal and glorious kingdom; where he lives and reigns with you and the Holy Spirit, one God, for ever and ever. Amen.[2]

Notes

Chapter 1: My Story

1. The term *transference,* of course, cannot be found in the Bible.

2. See Isaiah 53:4–5.

3. Several passages in Scripture speak of the relationship between idolatry, demonic activity, and the carnal nature in human beings: Psalm 106:36–42; Psalm 115:4–8; Psalm 135:15–18; Isaiah 44:17–20; 1 Corinthians 10:19–21; Galatians 5:19–21; 1 John 5:21. A good example from literature of the way an idol is first idealized and then despised can be found in *Till We Have Faces* by C. S. Lewis (New York: Harcourt Brace Jovanovich, 1957).

Chapter 2: Defining Transference

1. Lake's insights may be found in his large tome, *Clinical Theology: A Theological and Psychiatric Basis to Clinical Pastoral Care* (London: Darton, Longman & Todd, 1966), which unfortunately is out of print.

2. Lake, *Clinical Theology,* 405.

3. David Benner, ed., *Baker Encyclopedia of Psychology* (Grand Rapids: Baker, 1985), 1173.

4. Ibid., 1009.

5. Ibid., 878.

6. Lake, *Clinical Theology,* 406.

7. Medical doctors report cases of transference wherein a patient becomes preoccupied with one of his own internal organs or body parts. He becomes fixated on what is wrong with it rather than facing what is painful in his emotions.

8. Dr. Peter Gott, "The Doctor Says," *Arlington Heights* [Ill.] *Daily Herald,* 20 October 1997.

9. Names have been changed, and each character is a composite of several people, as with subsequent stories in this book.

10. See especially Mark and Gigi's story in chapter 3.

Chapter 3: Replayed Memories

1. Sigmund Freud, "Remembering, Repeating and Working Through," in *Complete Works,* trans. Joan Riviere, vol. 12 (London: Hogarth Press, 1958), 147–56.

2. Ibid.

3. Freud noticed a peculiar quality of timelessness related to the awakening of unconscious impulses: "The unconscious impulses do not want to be remembered in the way the treatment desires them to be, but endeavor to reproduce themselves in accordance with the timelessness of the unconscious and its capacity for hallucination." Freud, "The Dynamics of Transference," in *Complete Works,* 108.

Chapter 4: Childhood Roots

1. Lake, *Clinical Theology,* 28.

2. Many children who suffer from intense genital tension in infancy and childhood will, as these feelings become more sexualized during prepuberty and adolescence, have difficulty with masturbation. The practice of masturbation in these cases has its roots in infantile separation anxiety. For more on this, see Leanne Payne, *The Broken Image* (Westchester, Ill.: Crossway, 1981), 59–60.

3. Lake, *Clinical Theology,* 10.

Chapter 5: Repression, Pride, and Self-Deception

1. Lake, *Clinical Theology,* 29.

2. Freud, *Complete Works,* 107.

3. See Philippians 4:8.

4. Josef Pieper, *About Love* (Chicago: Franciscan Herald, 1974), 32.

Chapter 6: Overt and Litigious Encounters

1. 1 Samuel 30:4. This story is described in 1 Samuel 30:1–31.

2. David Goetz, "Forced Out," *Leadership,* winter 1996, 42.

3. Leanne Payne, *Leanne Payne Newsletter* (P.O. Box 1313, Wheaton, IL 60189-1313), fall 1994.

Chapter 7: Covert and Factious Liaisons

1. For the full story, see 2 Samuel 13–18.

2. Goetz, "Forced Out," 42.

3. Payne, *Leanne Payne Newsletter*, fall 1994.

4. See 2 Samuel 15:11.

Chapter 8: Vicarious Transference

1. Payne, *Leanne Payne Newsletter*, fall 1994.

2. C. S. Lewis, *The Four Loves* (New York: Harcourt Brace Jovanovich, 1960), 113–15.

Chapter 9: The Unseen Battle

1. Thomas à Kempis, *The Imitation of Christ* (Chicago: Moody, 1981), 45.

2. See 1 Timothy 1:15–19.

Chapter 10: Dealing with Transference

1. For a thorough explication of the freedom of the human will to choose wellness, even in a condition of psychosis, see Viktor E. Frankl's *The Doctor and the Soul* (New York: Random House), 1986.

Chapter 11: Traps to Avoid

1. For instruction about the Christian's authority over sin and evil, see John 20:23; Luke 9:1; and Luke 10:18–19.

2. Lake, *Clinical Theology*, 1127.

Chapter 12: What to Do if It's You

1. For a practical and comprehensive book about setting up a prayer journal read *Listening Prayer* by Leanne Payne (Grand Rapids: Baker, 1996). See also chapter 6, "Listening for the Healing Word," in *The Broken Image* by Leanne Payne (Grand Rapids: Baker, 1996), 129–49.

Conclusion: A Happy Ending

1. *The Book of Common Prayer* (New York: The Church Hymnal Corp., 1979), Collect, Proper 21.

2. *The Book of Common Prayer*, Collect, Proper 27.

Valerie McIntyre has been the administrator of Pastoral Care Ministries, Inc., in Wheaton, Illinois, since 1992. Before this she served as coordinator of Partnership Ministries, Bibles for the World, for four years.

While a student at Wheaton College, Valerie led the student evangelistic team and began a student ministry to the homeless in Chicago. She graduated in 1988 with a B.A. degree in social science.

At the age of fifteen, through reading the Scriptures, Valerie experienced a dramatic conversion to Christ. In 1989 she attended a Pastoral Care Ministries conference led by Leanne Payne and for the first time found answers to a problem that had surfaced during college: a difficulty in relating to others.

In 1994 Valerie shared her story, "Overcoming Transference in Relationships," at a PCM conference in England. The response to her testimony there, and subsequently in conferences in the United States and on the Continent, has been profound. The book *Sheep in Wolves' Clothing* has evolved from telling her story and teaching lay people and pastors about the dynamic of transference in ordinary relationships.

Valerie is a gifted musician, singer, and worship leader. She is married to Mark McIntyre and they have one child, Charis Elizabeth.